The
Good Wife's
Guide

The Good Wife's Guide

Embracing Your Role as a Help Meet

New York Times Best-Selling Author

DARLENE SCHACHT

The Ministry of
Time-Warp Wife

All Scripture unless otherwise noted is taken
from The NIV Bible

The Good Wife's Guide:
Embracing Your Role as a Help Meet

Time-Warp Wife
Suite 5-1377 Border Street
Winnipeg, Manitoba
R3H ON1

Copyright © 2011 by Darlene Schacht
Printed and bound in Canada
ISBN 978-0-9780262-1-9

Cover design by Darlene Schacht
Foreword by Candace Cameron Bure

To Michael,
my God-given gift of a husband and dear friend.

And to my four blessings,
Brendan, Madison, Nathaniel and Graham.
It's a joy to be your mom.

CONTENTS

FOREWORD

BY CANDACE CAMERON BURE

MY GREATEST ROLE AS A WOMAN is joyfully serving my family, but I'll be the first to say, that I'm not always joyful about it. It's one of the most difficult roles in my life today.

I think there is a gap between what God desires for us, what we want for ourselves, trying to emulate what we see others doing, and the honesty in it all. I can get bummed out when I see a family from the outside who I think has it all together. If I compare it to my own life, I feel like I'm nowhere close to where I want to be! But I've realized that I have a choice—I can either feel defeated, or be inspired knowing that God only expects my best. My "best" may be different from another woman's "best," depending on where we are in our lives.

I know as a married woman with children, God desires for me to be the wife and mother He intended me to be. That's my first priority--to take care of my home, teach my children, and build up my husband into the man he's called to be. Those three things in itself are no easy task and are often overlooked in our society as a throwback, or as something the modern woman doesn't need to focus on as much. I beg to differ.

I believe that families would be stronger today if we as women took back our femininity and invested more of our strength and power in our family. Dare I say it's almost easier to climb the corporate ladder?

Each of us has a different set of circumstances that dictate the way in which we live our lives. It's a challenge to see beyond the fame, beyond the glory, beyond the next self-fulfilling goal and focus on being the best wife, the best mom, and the best caretaker of my home that my family could ever have. I'm no exception to any of that.

Being a woman is a powerful role that God has called each of us to, and I love the ways in which Darlene helps us focus on those priorities and live out our desire to be "The Good Wife."

I find joy in being a helpmeet because I know from God's blueprint for marriage in the Bible, He intended for two to become one. When Val and I got married, I became my husband's partner in life, and he in my mine. It didn't take me long to realize that my life was no longer just about me, but about *us*.

That meant I needed to become a helper to my husband so that we, as a team, can live out a victorious life through our faith in Christ.

Being Christians doesn't mean our lives will be easier, that we'll have less conflict , or won't experience ups and downs, but it does mean the way in which we handle the roller-coaster of life is different than today's popular psychologists' interpretation.

I love that I can honestly say my husband is the head of our household. For me, that equals security, that equals comfort, and that equals masculine strength that I don't have to try to have myself. Trust me--I'm no pushover or doormat. I love being a feminine woman whose voice is heard but I also love that my husband makes the final decisions.

That to me takes off a load of pressure from my shoulders and allows me to be the nurturer I am. I believe as women, we are innately designed to be caregivers, nurturers, and lovers, and when we stop standing on our self-righteous principles to seek God's word, we'll find joy in serving those roles where we never thought we could.

When a family unit functions the way that God outlines it in scripture where a man and woman are given separate roles, the family works like a well-oiled machine. God created man and woman *equally* but *differently*. He gave us separate roles that are of equal importance but different performance.

Just watch any cooking show on TV. How many head chefs are there? Only one--unless they are competing against each other. Take a look at "Iron Chef," does the executive chef need help? Of course, that's why he has a sous-chef, the second in command, the direct assistant to the executive chef. One fulfills the other and this wouldn't happen if the other weren't there for him.

It's kind of the same in marriage and the family unit. Val has strengths that I don't and vice versa. Our kids won't get the same kind of tender-hearted patience, love or nurturing from Val that they will from me. And in the same way, the kids won't get the same kind of discipline, tough encouraging love, and drive from me that they will from Val.

God created man and woman to be uniquely joined together as one, and we become one when we function the way He outlined it in scripture.

Candace Cameron Bure
CANDACECAMERONBURE.NET

INTRODUCTION
THE GOOD WIFE'S GUIDE

*Blessed is the home of a woman
who joyfully serves, offering gifts
by the work of her hands.*

~ *DARLENE SCHACHT*

BEFORE WE GET INTO THE BOOK, I'd like to tell you what I
believe and what I stand for so that you will better understand
the heart of my message and what drives me to live as I do.

I love all things vintage: clothing, ornate furniture, dishes,
and strong family values. I cherish the days when giving one's
word meant something to her in this life; when the sanctity of
marriage was reserved for a man and his wife. When women
were *women* and men were just *men*. When the only *choice*
society offered was 'life.'

I cherish vintage values, and yet I understand they are
simply a means to an end. Yes they are to be cherished, but
unless I couple those values with strong conviction based upon
the Word of God and what is right in His sight, they are nothing
but tradition, custom and practice.

Good values are the roots that help little ones grow. They are
the threads that weave into the fabric of friendship. They are the
strands that bind one man to his wife. They are of great worth,

but the fruit we produce as a result of those values depend on the beliefs that are backing them up.

What I Believe

I believe that the Bible is the inspired word of God. My goal is to seek the will of God in every area of my life, and in doing so scripture isn't up for debate.

I believe that I was created to be my husband's helpmeet, and that he is the principal figure in our home. I joyfully accept this role and honor it as divine appointment from God.

> *Wives, submit yourselves to your own husbands as you do to the Lord. For the husband is the head of the wife as Christ is the head of the church, his body, of which he is the Savior. Now as the church submits to Christ, so also wives should submit to their husbands in everything.*
>
> EPHESIANS 5:22-24, KJV

I believe that I am called to ministry in my home. My role as their earthly shepherd includes nurturing our children to grow physically, spiritually, and mentally, nudging each little lamb should they stray.

As a Christian, I accept the Word of God to be true, and each time I apply it to my life I quickly discover that there is a good reason God put it there. His wisdom exceeds mine.

Does this mean that I am a doormat to my husband or that I'm compromising my beliefs in any way? Absolutely not—I'm reinforcing them. I'm living out my faith which is backed by belief. I'm happily choosing to be my husband's helper because faith powers every decision I make.

I believe that I was created with purpose, and in living out our purpose we discover a peace which passes all understanding through Jesus Christ our Lord.

The Good Wife's Guide

About a year ago, I came across a copy of what is called, "The Good Wife's Guide." It looked to be a photocopy of an article published by "Housekeeping Monthly," in May of 1955, but upon closer inspection, I got to wondering if the article might be a hoax. I recognized the photo as one I had previously seen on the cover of John Bull Magazine.

Wikipedia writes, "According to snopes.com, the wording "The Advertising Archives" located on the right side of the image suggests a fraud, since the Archives itself was not started until 1990."

So was it an email hoax? More than likely it was.

I got to reading the satirical article and so many of the points that it had were the same ones I stress through my ministry. In particular an article I wrote titled, "My Desire for Curb Appeal," in which I encourage wives to joyfully serve their families.

I clicked through several of the links online, and nearly everywhere the "guide" was posted, it was up for much ridicule.

The sad thing in all of this is that our role as a help-meet is being diminished by popular opinions that would rather scoff at good family values than face the truth of God's word.

> *Wives, submit to your husbands as to the Lord. For the husband is the head of the wife as Christ is the head of the church, his body, of which he is the Savior. Now as the church submits to Christ, so also wives should submit to their husbands in everything.*
>
> EPHESIANS 5:22-24, NIV

I've decided to resurrect the "Good Wife's Guide," in my own words, and according to the role that I hope to fulfill in my life. It is no longer a satirical piece written to mock the role of a help-meet, but rather a guide that leads women toward a noble character and good family values. It's time that we took a stand for family values that serve to grow and protect the family unit as God designed it to be.

CHAPTER ONE

LEARNING TO MANAGE OURSELVES

Purpose is found in those quiet moments when no one but God sees the work of your hands.

~ *DARLENE SCHACHT*

FIFTY-PLUS YEARS AGO, WHEN PARENTS WERE raising twelve children or more, a woman's place was in the home, while her husband was the sole financial provider. In today's world where many families rely on the income of both parents, many women are saying they have too much on their plate.

Having a family and a career is common, but hard to achieve. Combine that with a passion to raise a healthy, *close-knit* family, and you have some decisions to make. What do I cut? What do I keep? How can I be a good wife?

Titus chapter two exhorts women to love their children and to be keepers of the home. My hope is to enforce that message while teaching you how to do it with joy.

Now before you jump to the conclusion that this book is a manual for the "stay-at-home mom," let me say this SAHMs and working moms alike can both take joy in serving their families and glean from the lessons herein.

My passion is to encourage women to love and serve their families in hopes that we will all strive to keep our priorities straight. In doing so I'll offer you reasons for achieving a well-managed home backed by scripture and gleaned from experience. As well I'll provide you with detailed schedules for practical application.

My goal is to encourage you to make faith and family your first priorities from a place of sacrificial love. Whether that means that you are working inside or outside of the home will depend on the choices you make according to your own set of circumstances.

For the past sixteen years I've been blessed with employment opportunities through which I can set my own hours and work from our home office. But as I've pointed out--this is a *blessing* and I understand that it's not feasible for every mom. Unless I'm walking in your shoes I can't say what is driving you to choose your path or where your priorities lie. I can only hope that your decisions are grounded in faith.

Here is a letter I received from a reader along with my thoughts on "working" moms.

Dear Darlene,

Daily you inspire women to draw upon the Lord for their strength and defy recent conventions by being submissive (NOT the same as being a doormat) and serving.

My marriage was a world filled with abuse and adultery, which was obviously difficult, but I also got to be a stay-at-home mom for a few years. While it was never an ideal situation, I did not realize until I went back to work, and left my husband, how much of a difference it made in their lives and mine that I got to be with them those years. I miss the time with them desperately, but single mommas don't get to stay at home (unless they're remarkably fortunate).

I have a theory. I think we have developed a society where a majority of mothers are caught in a "catch 22" of permanent mommy-guilt. If we choose to stay at home, we are scolded for not contributing to the household income and may have a tendency to feel under-accomplished. Should we choose to maintain careers outside the home, we must constantly feel the guilt of knowing someone else is raising our children for us while we miss out on their most precious and formative moments. I'm sure it's quite apparent which choice I would make if I had one...but I don't.

I might not be a wife now, but if the Lord wills it, I would like to be one again someday. I know the next time around I will choose a man with a strong faith and Christian values, and whether I work outside the home or not, I want to serve God and my family by fulfilling the roles of wife and mother to the best of my ability. Therefore, I will continue to read and glean inspiration from your daily efforts.

Sincerely,

Single Mom

Dear Single Mom,

Thank you for your encouragement, and fellowship in the faith.

This was heavy on my mind when I went to sleep last night, as I received a letter from another reader, also on the topic of moms working. She wondered why I didn't support working women more than I do:

> *You don't seem to blog about moms who like raising their children, but who also enjoy working outside their household in their chosen profession. I'm a mom and a professional, in that I work outside my home in my chosen profession because I like it... Perhaps there is room for stay-at-home moms and professionals who respect the stay-at-home choice, and also vice versa?*

That's a good thought, and one to be considered.

For me the bottom line is that I encourage women to make *family* their first priority and to serve them with joy, whether that means that they are working inside of or outside of the home will depend on individual families according to their circumstance.

In some cases, like yours, it's not possible to stay home, as you have a responsibility to feed your children and put a roof over their head. We aren't all blessed with the traditional situation of a working father that is able and willing to provide for his family. In fact since the women's liberation movement we've seen an increased number of women in the work force, and as a result men are competing to get good paying jobs.

If a woman chooses to work because she has a passion for what she does, I don't see anything wrong with that situation providing that her primary passion is to her family. If we send our children off to daycare because we want a bigger house, a cabin, a boat or more spending money, then we may be prioritizing those things over the value of spending time with our children. We should all search our hearts when making important decisions like this.

I could never stand in judgment of working women because I am blessed with a work-at-home job. Unless I'm walking in their shoes I can't say what is driving them to choose their path or where their priorities lie, nor would I want to.

Looking to scripture we see the Proverbs 31 woman selling fine linen to merchants, buying a field, and planting a vineyard. What we also see there is a woman who rises early to feed her household and whose children call her "blessed."

I won't stand in a position where I pat either side on the back for the purpose of stroking one's ego, as I'm sure there are a large number of stay-at-home moms who would rather sit down and watch soap operas then cuddle on the couch with their kids or pick up a broom.

Being a stay-at-home mom shouldn't be a badge that anyone wears with pride. I would rather that moms would take pride in quietly serving God and their family.

All I can do is encourage women to love and serve their families in hopes that we will all strive to keep our priorities straight.

> *And whatsoever ye do, do it heartily, as to the Lord, and not unto men; Knowing that of the Lord ye shall receive the reward of the inheritance: for ye serve the Lord Christ.*
> COLOSSIANS 3:23-24, KJV

Sabbath Vs. Slothful

Throughout this book, I'm going to talk about managing our time in the home well, but while we do that I'm also going to encourage you to take some time out for rest. Being slothful, apathetic, idle, or lazy should never be confused with enjoying some R&R. We learn from scripture that the Sabbath was created for man and that even God himself rested on the seventh day.

Rest and relaxation are both a vital part of a well-balanced life in the same way that fat is a necessary ingredient to our diets.

Certain fats, known as "good fats," help our body to absorb vitamins, and provide us with energy. In much the same way productive R&R helps us to absorb those life-lessons that need sorting out, while providing us with energy to take on new tasks.

Rest isn't a problem in itself, but our misuse of it can be. We all know how good it feels to pull the covers over our head and press the snooze button a few times, but I have to say that a productive day feels better.

Over sleeping is an indulgent activity that should be reserved for special occasion like Saturday mornings--not just because our parents taught us that it was a good thing to do, but because our mornings set the stage for each day. If we want to live productive lives then it's time to take the reins and start leading the way.

Up until now, many of us may have allowed our bodies to lead without question but if we want to be a good wife who manages her house well, then we must start by learning to manage ourselves.

CHAPTER TWO

BEING SELFISH IS NOT OKAY

WHILE SWITCHING CHANNELS ONE DAY, I happened upon an interview. Since they were talking about family, it caught my attention so I paused to listen.

"Family... children..." I heard those words. Could she have the same passion and convictions as I? I turned up the volume anxious to hear more.

Unfortunately what I heard didn't resemble Christian living by any stretch of the imagination. In fact it was so absurd that I turned the television off and considered cutting cable altogether. My stomach was in knots over the attitude of acceptance that prevailed in this interview and the fact that they let this guest have air time.

After working oversees for a few months, this woman simply decided that she didn't want to be a mother any longer. She walked away from her two children (ages 3 and 5) and her husband of 20 years to build a career. While away, she missed her kids, but she "didn't miss when they were throwing up seven times during the middle of the night, and getting a call asking, 'Can you wash pillows?'"

What has this world come to when children are discarded like items on a yard sale table? When we say, "I don't want to handle the responsibility that comes with being a parent, so I'll step away—while someone else carries my load."

It's one thing to buy a pair of boots and change your mind a month or two down the road; it's an entirely different thing to walk away from responsibility because life isn't what we hoped it would be.

"Everybody has their own choices," she said, "but my choice works for us and I think it's not so selfish for women to say 'okay, I would like to have my own priority, I would like to have something in my life. I would like to be able to do my job.'"

"Not so selfish?" Is she serious? That statement is the very definition of the word selfish: *Devoted to or caring only for oneself; concerned primarily with one's own interest, benefits, welfare, etc., regardless of others.* (Dictionary.com)

As wives and mothers we can and should have our own interests, but when our *primary* concern is our "self" to the point that we become our first priority, we have given in to a selfish nature that isn't lined up with scripture.

Unselfish Love

Everyone has the right to make their own choices—we do, but when those choices affect the welfare of children, we as a society should be moral enough to stand up against these ideas and teach women that being selfish is not "okay."

Titus 2 exhorts women to love their children and to be keepers of the home. That doesn't mean that we can't have our own interests or earn extra money, but it does mean that we are to prioritize family because that's what love does.

Love is not self-seeking. When you truly love someone you get up in the middle of the night to wash pillows, regardless of how much those sheets stink, or how tired you are.

Timothy writes to the church in respect to the care of widows. What he has to say speaks volumes to parents as well:

> *But if any provide not for his own, and especially for those of his own house, he hath denied the faith, and is worse than an infidel.*
>
> 1 TIMOTHY 5:8, KJV

The Problem – Or Is It?

In 1963, Betty Friedan published a book called *The Feminine Mystique*. For only .75 cents a copy, women would find the answers to "the problem that has no name." This book was the catalyst for the second--and what appears to be the most damaging--wave of women's liberation.

> *"The problem is always being the children's mommy, or the minister's wife and never being myself."*
>
> FEMININE MYSTIQUE, CHAPTER 1

Apparently there was a "problem" that was plaguing housewives of the day, and according to the author, this problem could be fixed. If women turned inward and began to focus on *their* needs, *their* careers, and *their* happiness, they would find the happiness and sexual fulfilment they had been missing out on all along.

Since the author wasn't able to give "the problem" a name--let me. It's called, "sacrificial love," and according to the Bible, it's the only love worth giving.

Love is patient, love is kind. It does not envy, it does not boast, it is not proud. It does not dishonor others, it is not self-seeking, it is not easily angered, it keeps no record of wrongs. Love does not delight in evil but rejoices with the truth. It always protects, always trusts, always hopes, always perseveres.

1 CORINTHIANS 13:4-5, NIV

Was there really a "problem" or were a few women creating an issue that didn't exist?

I pray that women today will step up and realize the fallacy that this teaching offers. Seeking fulfilment by putting our own needs ahead of others brings temporal highs that fade quickly.

If you're seeking true joy with long-lasting results, it can only be found by building virtue upon faith. That's where you'll find fulfillment, and that's where you'll find your true purpose in life.

Turning Back the Clock

I'm not always politically correct. But as you might have noticed, that doesn't stop me from sharing what I see as truth. I've been accused of singlehandedly turning back the clock on women's rights, and I can see where that accusation is coming from. Joyfully serving your family? Submitting to your husband? Letting *him* be the head of your household? These ideas are fading into the past as modern women would prefer to wear the proverbial pants in the family--or at least a matching pair.

I'd like to address the question on everyone's lips, "Why should husbands get the final say?"

I'll start by saying this; letting him have the final say doesn't mean that you can't have a discussion and share your ideas. A good marriage should have channels of communication by which husbands and wives both offer ideas and determine solutions.

There should be mutual respect where both parties give and take of each other's thoughts. And there needs to be an attitude of acceptance where both a man and his wife can offer their voice.

> *But at the end of the day, he gets the executive vote. But I would have you know, that the head of every man is Christ; and the head of the woman is the man; and the head of Christ is God.*
>
> 1 CORINTHIANS 11:3, KJV

There's a reason why this works out for the best, and that reason has a lot to do with the fact that men and women are wired differently. It's a scientific fact that we have differing chromosomes, we are shaped differently and we deal with a monthly cycle including PMS. We are generally more sensitive, and as much as we hate to admit it--we cry.

Women have the ability to keep their emotions in check, don't get me wrong. I'm not saying that we fall apart as soon as the going gets tough. But what I am saying is that at the end of the day, women are more likely to suffer emotional turmoil while men stop to consider logistics.

However, more importantly than the obvious fact that men and women are different, the reason we submit to our husbands is because we are commanded in scripture to do so. God's wisdom doesn't always sit right with mankind, and it doesn't have to. Faith tells me that His wisdom exceeds mine and therefore I put my trust in His infallible Word.

Yes, that's politically incorrect, and to some it may be viewed as turning back the clock on women's rights. I get that. But really, what are the rights of a woman? Better said, what are the rights of mankind? Certainly we're given our constitutional rights, but who gives us those rights?

The way I look at scripture, we're given one right and only one--the ability to choose. Anything and everything else we are given is grace.

If that's turning back the clock on women's rights, then I say turn it back and keep turning it back until men and women accept scripture as truth that is both applicable and beneficial to families today.

> *And if it seem evil unto you to serve the LORD, choose you this day whom ye will serve... but as for me and my house, we will serve the LORD.*
>
> JOSHUA 24:15, KJV

CHAPTER THREE

GROUP YOUR LIFE INVENTORY

AS YOU'LL QUICKLY DISCOVER I'M LEARNING to lean just like you. I don't have it all together—nobody does. In fact there are times when I'm dropping the balls, and there are days when I cry out to the Lord because I know that I'm struggling and in desperate need of His help.

I understand what it's like to lose control of the mess and start feeling the stress, and so I'm writing this book for those women who are doing their best, but might find themselves failing time and again.

If you're one of those women, stop right where you are and consider this thought: *where you are today does not dictate where you will be tomorrow.* You have the ability to get your surroundings under control, to manage your home well, and find time to relax. My goal is to teach you how.

Let's begin this journey by looking at the following prayer: I'm using it as an illustration because it contains three vital points that we all should consider:

God grant me the serenity to accept the things I cannot change; courage to change the things I can; and wisdom to know the difference.

REINHOLD NIEBUHR

What's interesting about that prayer is that it teaches us to group our life inventory, to-do lists, busy schedules, workload, or whatever you want to call it into three categories:

1. *The things I cannot change.*
2. *The things I can.*
3. *The wisdom to know the difference.*

These are the three points that you'll find echoed throughout the pages of this book. We can't change the fact that we have laundry, dishes, school work, and cooking to do, but we can limit the time we lend to other things like television, internet, talking on the phone, texting, going out for coffee, and ministry outside the home.

Most women I know are busy. There are times when we take on too much. I've been there, and I'll venture to guess that many of you have as well. That's when it's time to step back and take an inventory. Sit down and decide what needs to stay and where you need to cut back. Doing this means that we must be willing to make some sacrifices whether personal or financial in order to keep faith and family as our top two priorities, in that order.

Discipline and Self-Sacrifice

My hope is to offer you life-lasting results. In order to do that, discipline and self-sacrifice must go hand in hand.

Let's start by learning what each of them are, and how they differ:

Discipline is "teaching and training yourself" which is where this book will be your aid. It will offer you ways train yourself in areas that tend to get out of control and it will provide you with schedules to keep you on track.

Self-sacrifice is much different. It's giving up our interests and desires for a cause. That "giving up" of ourselves is key to being a good wife, keeping an organized house, raising good children, and most importantly living a victorious life in Christ.

Most people look to discipline before they look at self-sacrifice hoping that a new schedule or book will do the trick. But just like those who go on crash diets, they return to the life they once had time and again because they aren't willing to *give up* anything. They want their surroundings to change rather than doing the heart work it takes to get from point A to point B.

If you ever read *Reshaping it All* a book I co-authored with Candace Cameron Bure, this concept might sound familiar to you. It's a vital step in reshaping any area of our life including our home and our marriage.

Set Priorities

Look at that prayer again. It says, "Wisdom to know the difference." The Bible tells us that if you lack wisdom ask God for it (James 1:5). Pray about your priorities and then set them according to the wisdom that you have been given.

Once your priorities are set, decide on the things that you need to keep and the things that you need to cut. Those things you need to cut should include physical junk (excess) as well as time wasters.

What things have to stay?
Where can we cut back or make changes?
What should our priorities be?

Answering those three questions should give us a good starting point.

Did you catch that definition? Self-sacrifice is giving up our interest and desires for a *cause*. And how do we determine the cause? We apply wisdom.

We need to decide once and for all what things are important to us and then set our priorities wisely. If a clean house is important to you, and your house is a mess then I'm going to step out and guess that it's not a priority to you.

But let me say that's not always a bad thing. If you have a newborn child, then taking care of that baby needs to be a priority and as a result the housework might falter. If you are taking care of a sick parent, then again you might need to make that your priority. So what I am saying here is that our priorities won't be the same as the next person--that's just how life is.

But babies and sick parents aside, consider your home. Are things ordered the way that they should be? If not, then ask yourself how much of a priority keeping the home is to you.

Be bold enough to ask yourself these tough questions too:

Do you prioritize the Lord enough to spend time in prayer, to read your Bible, to teach it to your children? We'll often hear women say that they love the Lord, but can't find time to read their Bibles.

I'm reminded of the year that Michael and I met. We both had full-time jobs and busy schedules, but because of our affection toward each other, we suddenly discovered that we had plenty of time to spend together. We had time because without even realizing it, we were prioritizing each other and making it work.

Where does your family fit in? Are you a stay-at-home mom so that you can care for your children or your internet friends? Are you working two jobs to provide for your family or to feed your lust for the world?

Because I'm a writer, I have an amazing schedule. I can choose when I want to work and how much I want to work. This is wonderful because I usually write when the kids are asleep or in school. Once the family is home I can shut my computer and give them my full attention.

But there are times when like everyone else, I get caught up in my work. I see opportunities and I grab them. Speaking engagements, radio interviews, celebrity books... all of those things are wonderful opportunities to be desired unless of course they draw me away from embracing my role of a helpmeet, being a good wife, and raising my children.

I can write about being a good wife until I'm blue in the face, but if I'm not living that role I'm nothing more than a clanking symbol.

That's where trust in God's plan must come into play. We have to believe that there is a time and a season for everything. Saying "no" today isn't about closing a door; it's leaving a room empty enough for God to fill it with something better.

CHAPTER FOUR

TIME WELL SPENT

WE STARTED GIVING OUR KIDS ALLOWANCE about four years ago according to age. It's not much, but enough to buy a snack, put a dollar into offering, and put a little away for something bigger like a video game or sports equipment. What I quickly noticed was that Nathaniel and Maddy were eager to spend their money on anything and everything they could get their hands on. They nickel and dime themselves at every turn until the last nickel and dime has been spent on junk. At the end of each week, they have little to nothing to show for their money. On the other hand, Graham is able to see the bigger picture and saves accordingly. He's interested in investing his money for bigger and better things like a trip or tickets to a hockey game. At twelve years old, he's even started talking about saving for a house, and after watching the way he disciplines himself, I don't doubt that he could!

In much the same way, some people look at the bigger picture and invest their time accordingly while others waste the time they have. There are a number of reasons that we waste time, some of which are:

- We're lazy
- We're unfocussed

- We're disorganized
- We lack moderation
- We're apathetic about the future
- We lack understanding and wisdom

We're all given the same amount of hours in each day, but those who manage their time well accomplish so much more than those who waste time surfing the net, watching television, talking on the phone, or sleeping in late. Those things aren't a problem unless they consume too much of our time. The goal is to be moderate in *all things* so that we're living a balanced life.

I'm reminded of the parable of the talents in Matthew chapter 25. A certain man went on a journey, and while he was away he distributed his wealth to each of three servants. Two servants invested their money (referred to as talents), while the third servant buried it in the ground. When the master returned, two of the servants had a good return on their investment which they were able to offer their master, while the third servant did not.

What we see here is that one servant was lazy, and as a result, his talent was taken from him and given to the servant with greatest increase.

If we're seeking a life of contentment and peace, we can't bury our heads in the sand while life passes us by. Those who seek to be a good wife soon realize that conscious living and practice are required of us. We invest in those things that are given to us from the Lord, including our time.

Here's the thing... when we think about time management we begin to focus on the time-wasters that surround us like television, internet, and the telephone. But the bottom line is that change begins in the heart where a battle is constantly taking place.

Our flesh wrestles with our spirit as it attempts to get its own way. Meanwhile the Spirit directs us to value God and our family, to prioritize them above everything else, and to avoid the tendency we have to be lazy.

The question is, which one do you choose?

The greatest investment that we can make is living a purposeful life in everything that we do.

Be self-controlled and alert. Your enemy the devil prowls around like a roaring lion looking for someone to devour.

1 PETER 5:8

Self-Imposed Pressure

Do you ever feel overwhelmed by the clock? That regardless of how good your intentions may be you never seem to get enough done? And if you do get caught up, you can't seem to stay there? There's a never ending rotation of dishes, there are always more tummies to feed, and the laundry pile is replenished on the hour…

Here's an interesting statistic: 70% of employees work beyond scheduled time and on weekends; more than half cited "self-imposed pressure" as the reason.

(SOCIETY FOR HUMAN RESOURCE MANAGEMENT, SPRING 2009)

Although many of my readers including myself are stay-at-home moms, I found that statistic to be an interesting one, because I think that "self-imposed pressure" is a common trait in many of us.

My husband will be the first to tell you that I work great under pressure. I can balance 52 balls at once, but put one task in my hand and I'm dropping it left right and center. The concentration and motivation to get the job done isn't fueling my fire as effectively as when I'm put under pressure.

That's not a good thing because when I am under pressure I give less time to my family, and I tend to sleep less which makes for a grumpy wife in the morning.

Go to the Ant

What's the solution? The Bible tells us to observe the ant…

> *Go to the ant, thou sluggard; consider her ways, and be wise: Which having no guide, overseer, or ruler, provideth her meat in the summer, and gathereth her food in the harvest.*
>
> PROVERBS 6:6-7, KJV

There are two kinds of women in this world, one who much like the ant plans wisely, and one who flies by the seat of her pants hoping that her cards will fall into place. Flying by the seat of your pants is also known as "impulse," or acting without forethought.

Consider this: what happens to your body when you start eating impulsively? For many of us, we gain weight, we feel sluggish, and our health is impaired. So it is with life. Wasting time or being over committed can lead us to that place where we are feeling the weight of over-commitment, which is not the most comfortable shape to be in.

And much like a diet where we consider "calories in and calories out," we're dealing with "time in and time out." You are given 1,440 minutes every day—use them wisely!

In other words *plan* your day. Get up in the morning pull out a pen and jot down the things that you'd like to see done. Secondly try to get those items on your list done early in the day in case things come up unexpectedly.

The other day I put off my housekeeping for late afternoon. It turns out that my mom decided to come over for a visit, and just before she did I got a call from the church that I had to run down there and take care of a minor emergency. By the time I finished with all of that, picked up the kids from school, ran to the supermarket, and got dinner started, it was about 5:00 and I was rushing around the house to get my cleaning done.

If I had taken a page from the ant, like the Bible suggests that we do, I would have been prepared. The house would have been clean when my mom came over, and I wouldn't have felt the stress that comes with work overload.

Planning Ahead

Planning ahead and setting priorities (whether they are of big importance or small) make for a happier mom! Planning eliminates the last-minute rush and setting priorities ensures that we don't impose as much pressure on our schedules.

If you'd like to start your own daily planner, here's what I suggest that you do. Either pick one up at the stationary store or make one of your own. All you need to get started is a three ring binder that holds 8.5 x 11 inch sheets of paper. If you can find one with a front pocket--even better as it is handy for storing receipts and important papers!

I have also created some daily printables that you can print off and use, which are available at my website: www. timewarpwife.com.

Each page has the monthly calendar at a glance, and the following sections to write in:

- To Do's - Things you need to do today
- Hope To Do's - Additional things you'd like to do if time permits
- Prayer Requests
- Reminders
- Bible Reading - What you plan to read in the Bible or a verse that comes to mind
- Groceries
- Thinking Ahead - Goals or future commitments
- People to Call

You can either print them off from my website or create your own, save the file on your computer and print the pages off as you need them.

CHAPTER FIVE

My Desire for Curb Appeal

IF YOU'VE EVER WATCHED HGTV, LISTED a home for sale or worked in a real estate office, you've heard the term "curb appeal." Curb appeal offers potential buyers a good first impression. It signals pride of ownership before they step through the door. It leads the guest to believe that the interior is well kept. It tells visitors that you care about the space in which you live.

It's a well-known fact to all of us that curb appeal can boost the beauty and value of one's home. In fact we had a friend who went as far as mowing his neighbors' lawn on each side of their house just so that the neighbourhood looked well kept. Incidentally they got an amazing return on their sale.

I miss the days when detail intensified the beauty of architecture, and when homes lining the streets were different one from another. When brass door handles, ornate mail slots and chiming door bells were the first things to welcome one home; when ornate windows framed each beam of sunlight that crept into a room until it found rest.

I live in a home, that I've taken special care to add character to. One particular hobby of mine has been designing our front yard with over-sized flower gardens and a cobblestone deck. Blue Adirondack chairs with striped pillows are a welcome sign to our guests, while a large floral wreath draws them toward our red door.

I spend hours on end planting my flowers, carrying stone, and pulling the weeds that threaten my plants--all this in hopes that I've welcomed my family and friends.

Of equal importance to me, however, is the welcome I offer my husband each day. From the moment he steps through the door, I want our house to feel like a home. I want life inside that door to be a haven of comfort and rest. And I want my husband to know I'm his help-meet.

When Daddy comes home, the children know that all activity ceases and quality attention is given to him. This curb appeal not only boosts the beauty of our relationship, it signals the pride of ownership that we share, and tells him that he's valued in our home.

Life can be busy and dinner time can be especially hectic, but with just a little effort on our part we can make a lasting impression. I know that even five extra minutes of my time can make the difference, and set the stage for a great evening. It's the little things that count.

Things I Do to Prepare for My Husband

We have all chores done before he walks in the door, and try to have things like the dishwasher and vacuum turned off.

I make sure that the television and stereos are turned off so that the house is peaceful.

If the kids are excited about something, I encourage them to wait about 15 minutes before they share their news.

I try to have dinner prepared before he arrives. For me it's not always cooked, but the preparation is usually done.

When I have problems to deal with, I wait until after dinner to spring it on him. I know that he's always happier when his tummy is full.

I always greet him at the door with open arms, a kiss, and a warm embrace.

I make an effort to look at him when he is speaking so that he has my full attention.

I close my computer if I'm on it, and if I'm chatting on the phone I'll try to end the conversation and call her back later.

Since curb appeal is the first thing that our husbands they see when they walk through the door, home-improvement is something all wives should consider. It's not a difficult task by any means, and the end result is well worth the investment we make.

Here are a few of the ways we can prepare ourselves and our house before our husbands come home. We all love to come home to a clean and tidy house, but let's not forget that husbands also appreciate a clean and tidy wife:

Take a look in the mirror an hour before your husband arrives to ensure that you are presentable. An hour allows ample time to hop into the shower if need be.

Go light on the perfume, but use great smelling soaps, shampoo, and antiperspirant so he'll want to snuggle up for the evening.

If you wear makeup, put a little on before he walks in. Your goal is to look happy and radiant--not done up.

Dress in feminine clothing. If he's like most men, he's more attracted to women than fashion, so do your best to wear styles, fabrics and colors that remind him you're a woman and not another one of the guys. Dress as well for him as you would for new friends.

Don't be angry if he's working late, instead show appreciation for long hours put in.

Have the kids wash their faces, and change their clothing if they are soiled from play before Daddy comes home.

Don't nag him about his day or try to reshape his bad habits. Work on your own and practice acceptance at all times.

A wife of noble character who can find? She is worth far more than rubies.

Proverbs 31:10, NIV

CHAPTER SIX

DOMESTICALLY CHALLENGED

I GUESS YOU COULD DEFINE ME as "domestically challenged." Cleaning and cooking have never come easy to me. In fact I was the one sister of six who had more clothes on the floor of her bedroom than I had in the drawers. Mixed in with the clothes you'd find a curling iron, Seventeen Magazines, makeup, note books, scraps of fabric, and art supplies. And while my sisters baked on Saturday mornings I slept off the late Friday nights.

I always had trouble hitting the hay, because I was constantly focused on a new project that had to get done. I can't count the number of Saturday's I started sewing a dress that had to be finished and ready to wear for church the next morning.

I later came to learn that I had ADHD with a tendency to over focus--a strong tendency. You see the rest of the world can fall apart around me while I'm working on a project and I probably won't notice until it's complete.

When I got married and started a family of my own, I realized that going to bed in the wee hours of the morning was rarely an option, and that I was facing a challenge when it came to housekeeping.

Not having the natural ability to organize myself, I managed to find direction in lists, schedules, and a few trusted recipes kept me on track until years of practice made me into the not-so-perfect housewife I am today.

The inadequacies of my life serve to remind me of Paul's letter to the Corinthians:

> *And he said unto me, My grace is sufficient for thee: for my strength is made perfect in weakness. Most gladly therefore will I rather glory in my infirmities, that the power of Christ may rest upon me.*
>
> 2 CORINTHIANS 12:9

Paul also points out in 1 Corinthians that he hadn't come to them with eloquence of speech, but rather in weakness, fear, and trembling. His preaching was a demonstration of the Spirit. In much the same way, Moses was unskilled in speech, but God appointed him as a leader.

> *But Moses said to the LORD, "If the Israelites will not listen to me, why would Pharaoh listen to me, since I speak with faltering lips?"*
>
> ~ EXODUS 6:12, NIV

Scripture after scripture we see God equipping those He calls. Whether He is calling you to be a missionary overseas or a keeper of your home, He is not calling the skilled, because as we know He is more than able to equip you at any time!

I've come to realize that being a keeper of my home doesn't require flawless perfection, and never has. It's all about being a gift to my family and to the Lord through the small sacrifices I've made with a willing heart:

- Getting up with a crying baby

- Making meals when I'm tired and uncreative
- Picking up after the kids
- Changing diapers
- Holding back anger to communicate well
- Cleaning up after the flu
- Offering a heart of forgiveness
- Waking early to make breakfast for the kids
- Scrubbing toilets
- Emptying garbage
- Teaching at the dining room table
- Going to bed last because I have to lock doors, tuck in children and turn off lights
- Dropping everything I'm doing to comfort someone's pain
- Driving, driving, and more driving
- Doing without so that the needs of our family are met

And the list goes on...

Domestically challenged? No problem. **"Sacrifice"** - that's what joyfully serving entails.

> *I beseech you therefore, brethren, by the mercies of God, that ye present your bodies a living sacrifice, holy, acceptable unto God, which is your reasonable service.*
>
> ROMANS 12:1, KJV

June Cleaver Syndrome

Through my readers I've come to learn that so many of us want to be a good wife and mother, but we can't help feeling that we never meet our own expectations, let alone anyone else's.

We make plans and schedules that we follow for a while with the best of intentions, but too often we give up and return to old habits.

I think that there are two things we need to consider here. One is what my sister Betty calls, "June Cleaver Syndrome." That is when our expectations are based on who we *think* we should be according to the high standards we see around us rather than *celebrating* the women that we were created to be.

June Cleaver Syndrome, develops when we're busy imitating someone else's expectations, rather than those that are a reasonable fit for our lifestyle. We have an idea of what a "perfect" mom should look like, but that image isn't anything near to the woman we are.

This desire for perfection can take the shape of anything from body image to the way we clean our house.

Let me give you an example. My sister Kathy is an organizational freak. Every nook and cranny in her house is well organized. Even her plastic bags are folded into perfect little triangles and carefully placed in their perfect little drawer.

I'm a writer. You won't hear the word "perfect" when it comes to describing my drawers. My bags are crumpled up and literally stuffed into a clothespin bag that I hang on the kitchen wall. I like a tidy house that is comfortable and clean, but if you pop in unexpected, you'll see a house that looks *lived in*.

With that said, let me address my second point: "self-control." The fact that I'm not a clean freak doesn't give me a ticket to be lazy in that area of my life. Scripture after scripture tells me that I'm called to be self-controlled in every area of my life.

*He that hath no rule over his own spirit is like a city that
is broken down, and without walls.*

~ PROVERBS 25:28, KJV

Ruling our spirit isn't any easier than training our body to run
a marathon. It takes patience, repetition, exercise, and action.
Those who are domestically-challenged need to stay focused
and avoid the temptation to let the mess get out of control.

I failed high school English, but failure doesn't dictate
my future. I have written two books, I own a self-publishing
company, and I'm a *New York Times* best-selling author. Failing
merely meant that *it wasn't time to give up.*

Rather than letting our past failures set the stage for our
future, they should be the very thing that tells us we need to
press on!

Here's a quote I wrote for a post on www.reshapingitall.
com. I love how it applies to every area of my life and sums up
the two points I'm making here:

> *What about those nights when you get so down on yourself
> because you made a mistake? Have you ever thrown the
> plan out the window because you didn't meet your own
> high level of expectation? We're not created to be perfect—
> we're created to press on!*

And let's not forget the words of Paul in his letter to the
Philippians:

> *Not as though I had already attained, either were already
> perfect: but I follow after, if that I may apprehend that
> for which also I am apprehended of Christ Jesus.*

> PHILIPPIANS 3:12

CHAPTER SEVEN

WHAT WILL THEY TAKE AWAY?

As my children are growing and watching every move that I make I'm careful to put my best attitude forward. Whether it's about waking early or hitting the books, I strive to reflect a level of enthusiasm in hopes that it might ignite a fire, and spur them on to embrace a good attitude of their own.

The first thing I've had to do is change my sleep patterns. We've gone from enjoying the lazy days of vacation to a structured school day all within a 24 hour period. This transition hasn't been easy since there was so much to do. I had to start getting up earlier again, getting four lunches made, and helping with homework. On top of that, my mom's been sick so I've been helping out over there a lot.

Life can be chaotic at times, but I've recently discovered that the key to controlling this chaos is *sacrifice.*

Why sacrifice? Let me explain.

The World English Dictionary defines "sacrifice" this way: *a surrender of something of value* as a means of gaining something more desirable or of preventing some evil.

The truth is that I don't want to go to bed earlier, and I don't want to get up early either, I'd rather lie in bed and enjoy the warmth of those incredible blankets for a little bit longer. But when I surrender my attitude and my desires to do the best thing for my family, I gain structure and discipline which work to calm the chaos. It offers us more time in the morning to get ready for the day.

Everything that I present to my family is a reflection of my heart. I can either show them that I value them by giving of myself with joy, or I can do it begrudgingly because it's something that has to be done.

Either path that I choose will be a learning tool that my children study as they grow. That's why I have to stop and ask myself, *What is it that I want them to see?* And then live accordingly.

Am I smiling? Am I affectionate? Do I show love, honor and respect to their father? Am I living a life of faith that they will be compelled to follow or one that will chase them away?

Some of those questions may appear to be minor considerations, while others are vital questions that we all need to consider. These are, after all, lives that have been placed in our care.

What do I have to offer them, and what will they take away?

Keep Your Attitude in Check

When I encourage wives to joyfully serve I'll often suggest that they look past the family. Look through them almost as if they're transparent—to where you see God, so that you're doing the work for the Lord. That's where you want your glory to be--not through the praise of mankind.

Everything we do should be for the glory of God, and so if you're cleaning for someone and you feel resentful, change your perspective on it. Say, "You know what? I'm doing this for the *Lord*, and I desire to please *Him*."

With that idea in mind, a fellow blogging friend told me that she used to post this verse on a card and hang it above her sink where she was doing dishes,

> *Whatever you do, work at it with all your heart, as working for the Lord, not for human masters, since you know that you will receive an inheritance from the Lord as a reward. It is the Lord Christ you are serving.*
>
> COLOSSIANS 3:23-24, NIV

I love that verse because it reminds me that even something as seemingly insignificant as doing the dishes can be done unto the Lord. After all, there's no better way to joyfully serve than with a heart of worship!

If that verse encourages us to joyfully serve, then why stop at the kitchen sink? Wouldn't it be uplifting to post scripture around the house as a reminder that we are serving the Lord with a heart of worship?

I think it would! So I dug out a few of my favorite scriptures that I thought might be a good fit around the house.

Here they are:

The Family Room:

> *Glorify the Lord with me; let us exalt his name together.*
>
> PSALM 34:3, NIV

By The Laundry Pile:

From the rising of the sun to the place where it sets, the name of the LORD is to be praised.

PSALM 113:3, NIV

On a Bedroom Door:

Unless the Lord builds the house, its builders labor in vain.

PSALM 127:1, NIV

Inside a Cupboard Door:

She rises while it is yet night and provides food for her household and portions for her maidens.

PROVERBS 31:15, NIV

The Front Entrance:

As for me and my house, we will serve the Lord.

JOSHUA 24:15B, NIV

The Night Stand:

Do everything without arguing and complaining.

PHILIPPIANS 2:14, NIV

Your Computer Monitor:

To be discreet, chaste, keepers at home, good, obedient to their own husbands, that the word of God be not blasphemed..

TITUS 2:5, NIV

The Bathroom Sink or Makeup Table:

Likewise, wives, be subject to your own husbands, so that even if some do not obey the word, they may be won without a word by the conduct of their wives, when they see your respectful and pure conduct.

1 PETER 3:1, NIV

CHAPTER EIGHT

REPETITION, PATTERN, ORDER

*She asks not how her behavior may please a stranger, or how another's judgment may approve her conduct; let her beloved
be content and she is glad.*

CHARLES SPURGEOON

After taking one look at the little cafe, I knew that I had to call my husband in from the car. The red vinyl booths, mini juke boxes at every table, and the checkerboard floor were a welcomed blast to the past. But what really caught my eye was the way that the vinyl bar stools lined up in perfect order.

Repetition, pattern, order. It was woven throughout the coffee shop, and it was breathtaking!

Equally as breathtaking is when one finds those three things incorporated into a family unit. It's been proven over and over that children respond to repetition. They learn better through repetition and their bodies even respond to repetition.

Take bed time for example. If we hit the hay at 10 pm every night, our body naturally prepares itself to rest at that time. And good habits like brushing one's teeth, or washing our hands are incorporated into our daily routine by constant repetition.

What about pattern? We see patterns everywhere in nature. Just take a look at any flower garden and we see repetitious patterns on nearly every plant, from the stems to the petals.

Families that set patterns for their children offer them a sense of comfort.

Eat - play- snack - sleep, might be one.

Chores - snack - homework - play, might be another. And disobedience - consequence, is yet another.

Order is one that many modern families prefer to ignore— at least family order as laid out in scripture. We see it in nature, we see it in business, we see it in politics, we even see it in the tri-unity of God, but time and again we fail to see it in the home.

When Dad is the head of the household, and mom is second in command we develop a sense of order. It doesn't make mom or the children any less important; instead it assigns an order of accountability to each person.

In an article published by actress/author Candace Cameron Bure, entitled "Submissive is Not a Four-Letter Word," Candace said, *"Think of it [a wife's submission] in military terms. You have a commanding officer and a soldier. There is a chain of command. Does that make the soldier's role less important? Of course it doesn't. If everyone was a commanding officer, there would be chaos.*

Same thing in your household; having two heads of authority doesn't work by design. Once a conflict arises, you will both stand on your principles until someone compromises, or worse--not, and the other will feel defeated. Most likely it will be your husband who'll do the compromising because it will be easier to give in than listen to his unhappy wife. This cycle will continue on in your marriage, only to have your husband feel he's incapable of making good decisions for your family, that you don't respect him, and ultimately find himself looking for a woman who will."

I love Candace's passion for being her husband's help-meet, and her understanding of family order, which is why I approached her about writing the forward for this book. It's refreshing to see modern women like Candace embracing their God-given role rather than trying to sweep it under the rug.

Stand By Your Man

There's no greater gift that a wife can provide to her husband than that role divinely fashioned by God.

> *The LORD God said, "It is not good for the man to be alone. I will make a helper suitable for him."*
>
> GENESIS 2:18

Being a help-meet says that my husband is the principal figure in our home. It doesn't mean that our marriage isn't a partnership, or that I am less of a person in the eyes of God. I am equal in the eyes of God, but have a different job than that of my husband. In order for any company to run smoothly, there must be a chain of command. It's for this reason that large companies have a CEO, managers, assistant managers, employees, shareholders, etc. It works for organizations and families alike because it makes good common sense.

Tammy Wynette wrote a song in 1968 called, "Stand by Your Man." The lyrics are about love, understanding, and forgiveness in a relationship. This song was a catalyst for feminists who wanted to jump on the band wagon saying that it promoted domestic abuse. Anyone who comes out with a similar message of devotion is likely to face the same line of criticism by those who don't understand.

But abuse is not what I'm talking about. Letting a man physically or mentally abuse you is a separate issue altogether and one that requires intervention from skilled professionals. What I'm talking about is respect and order in the house. Look up the lyrics of that song sometime and you'll be reminded of the old-fashioned values that we've been conditioned to forget.

CHAPTER NINE

LAUGHING OVER SPILT MILK

*Where no oxen are, the crib is clean:
but much increase is by the
strength of the ox.*

PROVERBS 14:4, KJV

MY "CRIB" ISN'T ALWAYS IN ORDER, but walk into my sister Bonnie's house at any hour of the day and you won't find a shoe out of place. Same thing with my sister Kathy. In fact Kathy told me yesterday that she "folds" her underwear before putting them in the drawer.

I like a tidy house, but with four kids around I don't take the time to fold panties, like I used to. Actually I don't think I ever did. But I remember a time when I would deep clean the house and it would look just as clean four days later. Those were the days before kids.

These days, maintenance takes more time than deep cleaning ever did. Ten minutes after I clean the house it's right back to where I started, unless I'm on them every minute, making sure they clean up after themselves. You wouldn't believe what's growing in a cup in our bathroom—gummy bears! Nathaniel wanted to see how large they'd grow in a cup of water. Apparently they grow a lot!

But I'm blessed. Life is messy, and I wouldn't have it any other way. Busy children trump an immaculate house any day of the week. Does it really matter that my carpet has a juice stain on it, or that my cupboard drawer no longer works because Graham thought it was a stepping stool? Things can be replaced, but nothing can replace the feeling of "home" that one gets when a house is bustling with children.

A Season for Everything

Don't get me wrong. I see the importance of cleaning our homes, and believe that it's an essential part of ownership. It creates a comfortable atmosphere for the ones that we love, and helps to bring order to our home. But there are still those times when it's okay to laugh over spilt milk, put whip cream on your chin, and climb up on the cupboards to roll dough with your mom. That's what living is all about.

While my kids are young and busy, and while I'm picking up after their every move, I'm reminded of the following scripture:

> *There is a time for everything, and a season for every activity under the heavens: a time to be born and a time to die, a time to plant and a time to uproot, a time to kill and a time to heal, a time to tear down and a time to build, a time to weep and a time to laugh, a time to mourn and a time to dance, a time to scatter stones and a time to gather them, a time to embrace and a time to refrain from embracing, a time to search and a time to give up, a time to keep and a time to throw away, a time to tear and a time to mend, a time to be silent and a*

*time to speak, a time to love and a time to hate, a time
for war and a time for peace.*

ECCLESIASTES 3:1-8, NIV

Looking back on my marriage of 23 years I see that to be true.
There have been tough times, and there has been laughter. We've
seen death and experienced life. We've experienced the strain of
unemployment, and the success of a growing business. We've
shared joy and we've shared sorrow. It's true.

And with that I also see that, "He has made everything
beautiful in its time." (verse 11)

CHAPTER TEN

BIBLICAL SUBMISSION DEFINED

*God speaks with authority on every
subject including marriage, and
His advice trumps Oprah's every time.*

KIRK CAMERON

MY SISTER HAD AN INTERESTING CONVERSATION with a woman at work. They were reading an article in our local paper about my ministry when this woman stopped short at the word, "submission."

Raising her head from the page, she asked my sister, "She doesn't really believe this, does she?"

This is the common reaction I get. People would rather see that word tucked away nicely in scripture where they feel it belongs, rather than exposing it to a modern society.

Scripture isn't a candy bowl by which we pick and choose our favorite words hoping to satiate our palette. It's a well-balanced diet of truth which is difficult to swallow at times, but nevertheless it brings nourishment to our soul.

I liked my sister's answer, which was this. "Yes, she does believe that, but do you really understand what submission means?"

Look carefully at the way that John Piper explains it, "Headship is the divine calling of a husband to take primary responsibility for Christ-like, servant leadership, protection and provision in the home. Submission is the divine calling of a wife to honor and affirm her husband's leadership and help carry it through according to her gifts."

Submission doesn't mean that we're weak-minded, feeble, or frail. It means that we're empowered by choice, and that we're dedicated to esteeming others higher than ourselves.

We teach our children to take the high road when the going gets tough—to walk away from a fight. We tell them how much more blessed it is to *give* than for one to receive. We enforce the golden rule of "love your neighbor as yourself." But we can't accept the reality that loving someone as much as we love ourselves means that we must be willing to sacrifice your own desires for their happiness.

> *Do nothing out of selfish ambition or vain conceit. Rather, in humility value others above yourselves, not looking to your own interests but each of you to the interests of the others.*
>
> PHILIPPIANS 2:3-4, NIV

Here's an example. Consider a woman who is conscious of her health. She lives a lifestyle that will benefit her rather than one that fulfills her desire. She gets up at 7 am to work out because her body is under submission to her flesh. Does this mean that she's any weaker than someone who lives impulsively? Absolutely not. Her ability to submit to good choice is the very thing that makes her strong.

The benefits of living in submission to your husband are many, and that's a good thing. But really the bottom line isn't whether it benefits us or not. That's where society errs. They measure God's wisdom against their own, accept those ideas they like, and reject those they don't.

> *All scripture is given by inspiration of God, and is profitable for doctrine, for reproof, for correction, for instruction in righteousness: That the man of God may be perfect, thoroughly furnished unto all good works.*
>
> 2 TIMOTHY 3:16-17,KJV

The Whole Truth and Nothing But the Truth

The word "submission," isn't acceptable in this day and age. In fact from what I've seen, it's deemed rather offensive to most non-believers. Christians on the other hand accept the term, but some kindly suggest that we be hush-hush about such matters.

That's odd, because from what I've read, the disciples weren't quiet about it, in fact the word "submit" appears in the Bible several times as we are commanded to submit to our husbands, submit to our God, submit to the ordinances of man, submit to our elders, and submit one to another.

I won't sugar coat or water down the commandments of God to tickle the ears of the weak. Majority doesn't rule, and popularity doesn't hold the deciding vote.

Titus 2:5 tells older women to instruct younger women to be "obedient" to their husbands. The Greek word for "obedient" is hypotassō - Strong's Concordance G5293:

> *This word was a Greek military term meaning "to arrange [troop divisions] in a military fashion under the command of a leader." In non-military use, it was "a*

voluntary attitude of giving in, cooperating, assuming responsibility, and carrying a burden."

It's the same word we see being used here:

> *Wives, submit yourselves unto your own husbands, as it is fit in the Lord.*
>
> COLOSSIANS 3:18

With that in mind, what does a submissive relationship look like? Does that mean that we have an over-bearing husband and a timid wife?

Absolutely not, the ideal picture of submission is that of two people loving and serving each other.

Consider this, Paul writes to the Ephesians in chapter five instructing husbands to love their wives "as Christ loved the church and gave himself for it." So what we see here isn't the role of a tyrant, we see a man who spent his last hours washing the feet of his disciples. He came in the form of a servant and humbled himself before man and God.

> *Let this mind be in you, which was also in Christ Jesus: Who, being in the form of God, thought it not robbery to be equal with God: But made himself of no reputation, and took upon him the form of a servant, and was made in the likeness of men: And being found in fashion as a man, he humbled himself, and became obedient unto death, even the death of the cross.*
>
> PHILIPPIANS 2:5-8

Some of us want nothing more than to point this out to our husbands so that he's pulling his weight. It's so much easier to instruct others than it is to instruct ourselves--to work on improving their walk of faith rather than improving our own.

But the truth is that my ministry isn't for the purpose of instructing your husband or my husband on how to be Christ like. My role as a woman is to encourage you to be the best wife, mother, homemaker, or hopeful bride you can be. In doing so I'll ask you to swallow your pride from time to time. I'll encourage you to walk in humility, esteeming others higher than yourself. I'll pray for you as you carry your cross. And I'll rejoice with you as together we joyfully serve!

CHAPTER ELEVEN

NO NEED OF SPOIL

As a keeper of my home, I am entrusted with the responsibility of taking care of the things that we have. My husband supports our family financially, so if I make a big supper and leave the leftovers on the cupboard to spoil overnight I'm wasting money that he has laboured for. Or for example, if I'm not diligent to turn off the lights when I leave a room or turn down the heat at night, I'm showing disrespect to my husband and setting an example of disrespect to my children.

When I ask my husband to pick up milk on the way home, he can trust that I don't have a jug full in the back of the fridge turning green.

In the same way, we take care of our things to honour God. Everything we have is a gift from Him. Whether your husband takes home the paycheck or you both do, all that we have comes from above.

The way to avoid waste is by making an effort to take care of our things, and by avoiding the temptation to be lazy. It feels like I'm doing something productive when I'm on the computer, but too often I get drawn away by the temptation to vedge out on facebook, twitter, and blogger. Not that those things are wrong necessarily, but the time we spend online needs to be kept in check. Idleness, that takes us away from work that needs to be done, is in every way a form of laziness.

> *He also that is slothful in his work is brother to him that is a great waster.*
>
> PROVERBS 18:9, KJV

I've come to learn something about housekeeping over the years. The more dis-organized I am, the more things get damaged, lost, moldy, rusted and forgotten. In fact I remember going to the hardware store about five years ago to load up on baseboards, only to later find out that we had a stash of them under the crawl space. That alone could have saved us about a hundred dollars.

If I could tally up all of the little things over the years, such as ribbons, buttons, socks, and pens that I've purchased because I "thought" I needed another, or bits of green cheese I threw out, I'd probably discover a tidy sum of money that could have been saved for retirement.

It's really the little things that get us, since the big things are hard to miss. Most people don't step over baseboards for five years and replenish their stock, but we all have those drawers full of twist ties, post it notes, pencil crayons, glue sticks, lost keys, and paper clips, don't we?

I thought I was doing well last September when it came time to buying school supplies. I recycled whatever I could and saved us some money. But somewhere around the end of October I happened upon a bag on the top shelf of Graham's closet that contained most of the items I bought.

I once knew a family who didn't waste one bite of food— not one. Even if that food was a package of crackers from a restaurant, the mom would put the crackers in her purse to take home. And if the crackers got crumbled, she'd use them for bread crumbs (mind you they rarely ate out). On one occasion I was standing in her kitchen when her daughter pulled out half of a piece of licorice that she had been hanging onto for weeks. She was wondering what she might use it for; tea perhaps? Tossing food in the trash was not an option.

I don't think I'd take things as far as they do, but I do see the reasoning behind it. By cherishing the gifts that we have--even in small acts of stewardship, we reflect a heart of appreciation, respect, and reverence.

Do you love the giver? I thought so. Then let's show Him, by loving His gifts.

The heart of her husband doth safely trust in her, so that he shall have no need of spoil.

PROVERBS 31:11

CHAPTER TWELVE

LIVING IN UNITY

Perfect love is perfect self-forgetfulness.
Hence where there is love in a home,
unselfishness is the law.
Each forgets self and lives for others.

J.R. MILLER

Together we stood at the altar; me dressed in fine vintage lace with white leather pumps, and Michael in a handsome new suit. He was the most incredible man I'd ever met in my life, and still is. Vowing our love one for another those 23 years ago, we were eager to accept the idea that we were no longer two, but one.

But at the beginning of creation God made them male
and female. For this reason a man will leave his father
and mother and be united to his wife, and the two will
become one flesh. So they are no longer two, but one flesh.

MARK 10:6-8

While we readily accepted those words, we had little understanding as to what they would require of us. Hearing words and living them out are very different when humanity comes into play. We humans tend to be self-centered and downright selfish at times, making the concept of unity about as easy as bathing an angry cat—let's make that ten.

It's easy to be of one mind when you adore someone so completely that you can't imagine living a minute without him. But the real test comes when the honeymoon is over, responsibilities set in, and petty arguments come up. I pray that they don't, but unfortunately couples who are dealing with life issues tend to get tired, irritable, and short tempered at times.

I once knew a couple who argued about the price of peppers for two days straight. Other than that, they were an incredibly happy couple, but somehow the topic of peppers managed to come between them that week.

What is an argument really? The word originates from the root word "arg" (as in argent) meaning "to shine." It doesn't make all that much sense unless we look at it this way: "One's desire to shine."

That's what an argument is really about: our need to shine, our need to be right, our need to be heard.

> *Do nothing out of selfish ambition or vain conceit. Rather,*
> *in humility value others above yourselves.*
>
> PHILIPPIANS 2:3

Humility, tenderness, grace… that was God's plan and intention for marriage when in Genesis 2:18, the Lord God said, "It is not good for the man to be alone. I will make a helper suitable for him."

But when sin entered the world, so did selfish ambition and pride. There was no longer a passion to serve one another, but a knee jerk reaction to protecting one's self.

God asked, "Have you eaten from the tree that I commanded you not to eat from?"

And Adam replied, "The woman you put here with me—she gave me some fruit from the tree, and I ate it."

Then the LORD God said to the woman, "What is this you have done?"

The woman said, "The serpent deceived me, and I ate." (Genesis 3:11b-13)

God asked them direct questions, but with each answer they shifted the blame away from themselves to another. In other words they both had a desire to shine.

How do we heal this? How do we move from a place contention to that place of unity where God desires our marriage to be?

We find the answers in Philippians 2:3-4:

> *Give up any selfish ambition or conceit, including your need to be right.*

Humbly value him higher than yourself. Don't focus on your own interests, but be sensitive to his.

> *Make my joy complete by being like-minded, having the same love, being one in spirit and of one mind. Do nothing out of selfish ambition or vain conceit. Rather, in humility value others above yourselves, not looking to your own interests but each of you to the interests of the others.*
>
> PHILIPPIANS 2:2-4

5 Ways to Handle Conflict in Your Marriage

Pray, asking God to take your burden. I say this often, because it's so important that we believe it. We can't change a person, but God can. Our job is to walk according to God's will in every situation, and He will do the heart work.

Stop looking over the fence, because green grass is temporal. As long as we're looking at other couples around us, we're always going to find what appears to be more fortunate couples than us.

In fact your best friend might have an incredibly handsome husband that does the dishes every night AFTER he runs her bath. (Ha!) But the truth is that even husbands are temporal. Unfortunately that relationship could be gone in a moment and all that is left would be dust in the wind. Life happens to all of us including death, poverty, sickness and loss, which is why it's important that we invest our hearts in the eternal joy that comes to those who seek God.

Our husbands are an extension of our relationship with God, not the root.

Look past his faults and focus on love. The characteristics of love are patience, kindness, having no envy, goodness, faith, meekness and temperance (self-control), which means that it takes a lot of doing on our part to love difficult people. But you know what? In doing so, you grow in virtue while at the same time you bring glory to God.

The other day I had to drop my son off at my husband's work to help out. The problem was that I was on my way to an appointment clear across the city and had to make a major detour in rush hour traffic. I knew that going to both places would mean that I had to drive about 3 hours—not thrilled. Meanwhile my son wasn't too excited about going to help Dad at work when he could be at home chillaxing in front of the TV.

This gave us both an opportunity to love. If love was supposed to be easy, it wouldn't need to be described as "patient."

The characteristics of love grow when they are exercised on a regular basis.

Be understanding of his faults. People are human, and therefore we are flawed and yes sometimes we're downright annoying. But consider this, Jesus didn't die for us because we were charming did He? He died for us because He was obedient to the will of the Father. People don't always deserve our love, but we give love in every circumstance because our ultimate purpose is serving the Lord.

We all have differing faults because we all process the world in a different way. We process our emotions in a different way too. So while some husbands might pay attention to their wives, other husbands might tune out the world and tune into the television.

Does that make him a bad person? Not necessarily. It could be a number of different things from immaturity to an inability to handle stress. We don't always know why people do the things that they do, because we've never walked in their shoes.

By working to improve our own faults we offer an example that they can learn by. Hopefully that example reflects both the love and life of Christ.

Keep the lines of communication open. A lot of women will say that their husbands don't talk enough, but yet he was plenty talkative while they were dating. What gives?

A nagging wife will often use methods of shame, blame, criticism and guilt to get her way, and as a result men build walls of protection around them. We don't mean to do it, but when feelings get hurt or when we feel neglected we tend to act out. Unfortunately nagging can become a habit for some. After a while, the methods of communication that once worked stop working, and the couple is left void.

If you want your husband to trust you with his heart as he once did, it's important to practice self-control, hold your tongue, and replace criticism with kindness. Listen when he talks and make an effort to show him respect.

All five of these steps seem as though they are intertwined, because they are. Each one of them call us to love as God would have us to love.

Out of curiosity, I looked up the word "love" at dictionary.com. I wanted to see how the world defines love compared to the way that God defines it. For the most part, the results I found were little more than passion, desire, and sexual attraction. That kind of love doesn't hold up when we're dealing with the real issues in life like poverty, cancer, Parkinsons, and Alzheimers, but unfortunately that's the extent of many relationships in our society today. And that's why so many relationships fail.

Love—the way that God intended it to be—calls us to embrace the same attitude as Christ; an attitude of humility, self-sacrifice, patience, and kindness. That's how we live out the truest form of the word. And that's how we turn a life sentence into a life worth living.

Building on Love

Many experts in the field of marriage say that the leading cause of marital breakdown is that of unrealistic expectations. Whether it is a Christian marriage or an unbelieving couple, we see this happening every day.

With that I'm reminded of a key principle that I learned when I was doing website design a few years back. It goes like this: the first question that a reader considers when they land on your site is, "What's in it for me?" If you can't supply the answer to them in 20 seconds or less, you will likely lose that reader to another website.

We're selfish beings born into sin, struggling against the flesh every day of our lives, and a big part of our struggle includes a strong desire for self-fulfillment. In other words we're born selfish.

Just look at any two-year-old and you'll see a child that is in the process of learning what sharing is all about. We come out of the womb screaming and asking ourselves, "What's in it for me?"

That's the same question that many of us take into marriage as we're seeking fulfillment, but soon after we say our "I do's" we realize that the day to day responsibilities and sacrifices required of us aren't what we expected.

Some of those unexpected surprises might include things like:

- Children are expensive
- Living costs are high
- You are arguing about petty things
- Your spouse has an irritating habit you never quite noticed before
- He doesn't understand you
- He doesn't pay enough attention to you
- You like different programs on TV and he holds the remote like his life is depending on it
- He's a slob
- Babies cry all night long and stay up all day
- There is more laundry than you ever dreamed possible
- Planning meals and cooking is time consuming

- You can't find enough time for yourself
- You don't get to spend every holiday with your parents like you used to
- His family is difficult
- Your mother-in-law is too involved

Realities like these have a way of wearing the shine off of a once gleaming *romance*, but don't let them get in the way of your *love* for a second! In fact here's what I suggest that you do: **consider it joy.**

If you haven't already, you can start by giving up on the question, "What's in it for me?" and replace the question with, "What can I offer?" Every time that you work through any of these obstacles with patience, humility, and kindness you are building and strengthening your bond of love. Think of these stressors as weights that are shaping your "marriage muscles." Just like any healthy muscle, your marriage needs strength training. Let's face it ladies, we all know that a muscle will not be strengthened unless it carries a weight or something bears upon it. Be willing to carry that weight and see how it promotes growth in the long run.

How many women have hit the gym with the mantra, "No pain, no gain!" and then walked away from a marriage because it wasn't all that she hoped it would be? Far too many, unfortunately.

On the other hand, those who stay the course and finish the race to the end, realize how beautiful love can be when two people work to strengthen and shape it.

Consider it pure joy, my brothers and sisters, whenever you face trials of many kinds, because you know that the testing of your faith produces perseverance. Let perseverance finish its work so that you may be mature and complete, not lacking anything.

JAMES 1:2-4, NIV

If you want to build a strong Christian marriage, start your fitness routine today!

CHAPTER THIRTEEN

THE TREASURE OF YOUR HEART

I RECENTLY GOT TO THINKING ABOUT authentic compassion. This idea of genuine love has been on my heart, as I've been guarding my mind against negative thoughts and training my tongue to offer positive praise.

I got to thinking about those things that I do in private, whether good or bad and began to realize that as much as we might try to fool people, we are far more transparent than we'd like to think.

Ever meet a person that you referred to as "genuine?" Chances are, they probably were.

> *A good man out of the good treasure of his heart bringeth forth that which is good; and an evil man out of the evil treasure of his heart bringeth forth that which is evil: for of the abundance of the heart his mouth speaketh.*
>
> LUKE 6:45, KJV

We see here that speech reflects the treasure of the heart, but I also believe that our mannerism, our smile and our eyes speak volumes that echo the message we store deep within.

Quietly Planting Seeds

There's something about privacy that brings out the worst in us. Most of us would be more than happy to lend a neighbour a helping hand, but few will be as generous with their time and compassion when no one is there to give praise.

There's a reason it's important for us to live righteously in private. First and foremost being that God sees everything and all things will be revealed in His time. But the second reason is that during those times of quiet decision, we are planting seeds that will grow in our heart.

You can't plant crab grass and expect daisies to bloom. The seeds that you plant and allow to take root in your heart will determine the splendour of the harvest you yield.

> *Finally, brethren, whatsoever things are true, whatsoever things are honest, whatsoever things are just, whatsoever things are pure, whatsoever things are lovely, whatsoever things are of good report; if there be any virtue, and if there be any praise, think on these things.*
>
> PHILIPPIANS 4:8, KJV

Last winter my parents woke up to find that their walk was shovelled for them, and they knew that one of the neighbours must have done it while they were sleeping.

It's interesting to note that they were able to pinpoint who the Good Samaritan likely was. It wasn't because he left a calling card on their door saying "Hey, look at me!! I just shovelled your walk, and you're welcome!" They knew who it was because of the genuine kindness they sensed in this man.

That's the message God is sending to us in Matthew 6, when Jesus says, to let our giving be in secret. Understanding the importance of the treasure within, He encourages us to love well.

> *But when you give to the needy, do not let your left hand know what your right hand is doing, so that your giving may be in secret. Then your Father, who sees what is done in secret, will reward you.*

MATTHEW 6:3-4, KJV

Let Your Intentions Be Good

The development of patience, sincerity, and kindness requires us to be conscious of the actions we choose. Whether in word or in conduct we have the potential to affect others around us and leave an imprint on their life.

Stop for a moment to consider what they see. Do you smile often enough? Do you respond to your children's desire to be heard and be seen with all eyes on them? Are you willing to forgive others when you have been wronged, or do you react in anger?

I came across this quote by Grenville Kleiser. It exemplifies the change I desire to be; the woman who stands beyond the window of each human eye, and reflects the love of God in all that she does--a servant ready and prepared for His work.

> *Let your intentions be good - embodied in good thoughts, cheerful words, and unselfish deeds - and the world will be to you a bright and happy place in which to work and play and serve.*

GRENVILLE KLEISER

How much greater is our gift when those intentions are backed by a desire to serve an almighty God? When our purpose is grounded in Him?

Max Lucado once wrote, "A woman's heart should be so hidden in God that a man has to seek Him just to find her." And I believe that when a woman is truly abandoned to God, a husband, enthralled by her heart, is stirred to embrace Him.

Karen and Brian

Let me tell you about Karen. I met her several years ago when we attended the same "Ladies Morning Out" group. She was a blessed soul who has now gone on to live in the arms of Jesus, or as Karen would say, "In the arms of *my* Jesus!"

Karen's husband Brian wasn't a Christian, and so each and every Tuesday morning we prayed for his salvation.

What I liked most about Karen is that she was living a life that reflected her love for Jesus. In other words, she did more walking than she did talking when it came to the things of the Lord. Her deepest desire was to see her husband experience salvation and the kind of joy that only comes through living a life abandoned to God. But she wasn't about to push him.

While Karen made Brian's lunches, she inscribed, bits of scripture into the mayonnaise. She prayed over this pillow while he was out, and most importantly she laid her burden at the feet of Jesus so that her husband might be won over by her behavior rather than a string of empty words.

Within a year, Brian was ushering at the church. He didn't just offer lip service to the Lord; by his wife's example he surrendered all that he was at the foot of the cross, and was never the same after that.

They've both passed on from this life—each within months of the other; both sooner than their age would dictate. Looking back at how quickly that all came and went, one has to wonder where Brian might be today had it not been for the quiet spirit of one woman faithful to God. One also has to wonder the impact that our lives can have when, with a quiet spirit, we walk the walk more than we talk.

The bottom line is that we'll never have the power to affect another person until our words become flesh. Until we're living in complete submission to the Lord so that the treasure of our heart becomes a compelling force that not only reflects what we believe, but also stirs people to embrace the God that we serve!

Here's a letter I got from a reader…

Dear Darlene,

I just read two of your articles this morning and I felt that the Lord was using both of them to minister to me personally. One of the things that you said that really drew my attention was…

"We see here that speech reflects the treasure of the heart, but I also believe that our mannerism, our smile and our eyes speak volumes that echo the message we store deep within."

"Our smile"… I don't have one anymore.

Two years ago… on our youngest daughter's wedding day, no less… I lost the second of two teeth in the front of my mouth. We don't have the money to fix them (I need to get two pulled and a flipper made--that's the plan anyway), but ever since that day, I've clamped my mouth shut and am embarrassed and ashamed to open it--and I DON'T smile anymore. Because of this I am ashamed and embarrassed to even talk to people in person.

I'm sorry, I know that there's really no answer to this, but this is one of those issues that I haven't talked to anyone about other than my husband. And he just says not to worry about it... that I'm "beautiful" the way I am and that God will provide when the time is right, which is true--I know He will.

But, Darlene, it's been TWO years now! HOW can I overcome the shame and embarrassment of this without having the problem fixed? And is it prideful of me to be like this?

I'm such a mess. Forgive me. I don't mean to be so negative and needy. I try so hard to overcome and I just don't seem to make much progress at times. Forgive me if I've done anything wrong by bringing this to you. I love you and I value your opinion.

Sincerely,

Wanting to Smile Again

⌒

Dear Wanting to Smile,

I think we can all relate to you because the truth is that we're all "flawed" in some way or another (if we can even call it a flaw). In fact one major imperfection I have is a partly paralyzed arm that's been this way since birth.

Practically speaking, here's what I suggest: **Practice.** Force yourself to do it until it feels natural to you. I'm uncomfortable with my arm, and every year I feel a twinge of embarrassment when the hot weather rolls out. I know that I'll be wearing short sleeves and going to the beach and I can't imagine having my arm laid bare. But I force myself to wear t-shirts and after a while I forget that I was ever worried about it at all.

Here's the thing--when you're smiling, people aren't looking at your teeth. They aren't even looking at your mouth. They are absorbing the energy that you are sending through your smile. This energy is what I'm talking about when I say "live an authentic life."

If a person doesn't receive the warmth of your smile, the problem isn't with you, it's with them. So really the issue isn't yours to deal with—it's theirs.

Consider this--what do you see when a baby smiles-- happiness, beauty, and joy? Or do you focus on the fact that they are short, bald, chubby and toothless? We all see the authentic treasure of their precious little heart, because beauty comes from within.

That's why your husband can say "You're beautiful." Because he sees your beauty, and don't kid yourself--others are seeing it too!

A merry heart maketh a cheerful countenance: but by sorrow of the heart the spirit is broken. ~ Proverbs 15:13, KJV

I'm reminded of my friend, Mandy Young. She's a one legged girl, and she dances—yes dances--and she wouldn't have it any other way. While there are people who complain they can't "Zumba" Mandy says, "You're not going to let a one legged girl show you up, are you?"

Her zest for life is incomparable:

I must get asked 5 times a day, "What happened to your leg?" And I get to share the amazing journey that I have been on and share my love for the Lord with everyone that asks! If I hid behind "normal" I would never get to do that.

I am so happy for the way He has made me and I kinda hope I'm still one legged in Heaven too.

MANDY YOUNG

Not smiling because you are missing some teeth, would be like Mandy not dancing because she's missing a leg. Not only would Mandy miss out on a blessing, the people around her would miss out on one too.

Don't wait for a cosmetic smile to define you. Embrace what you have today, and use it for the glory of God.

You are loved by an almighty God,

Darlene

In this chapter we've talked about the importance of inner beauty, now let's move on to the next chapter where we look at several ways to enhance inner beauty without swallowing makeup!

CHAPTER FOURTEEN

ENHANCE YOUR INNER BEAUTY

LIFE IS FUNNY, ISN'T IT? WE can be busier than a bee in a flower shop, but ask us to step outside and we can't do it without at least pausing for one final glance in the mirror. In fact I have a beautiful over-sized mirror, with a walnut frame, hanging right beside the front door for this very reason.

In this chapter, I want to take this idea of studying ourselves in the mirror, turn it inside out so that we're looking at things from the best perspective, and make this ritual an important part of our everyday lives.

What do I mean when I say "turn it inside out?" I'm talking about evaluating ourselves from the inside to see how we present ourselves as a wife and mother.

Most people present themselves beautifully to the outside world, but turn that person inside out and you begin to see what they're like behind closed doors. Speaking for myself I see plenty of room for improvement!

*Examine yourselves to see whether you are in the faith;
test yourselves. Do you not realize that Christ Jesus is in
you--unless, of course, you fail the test?*

2 Corinthians 13:5, NIV

Where do we start? The best source for improvement isn't found on Oprah or the Dr. Phil show, it's found within the pages of the Bible where God's will for mankind is clearly laid out in print. Sure it's easy to flip through channels hoping to glean motivation from a smooth talker in designer shoes, but God's incomparable wisdom exceeds "The View" of mankind any day of the week.

And yes--His wisdom is so much greater than anything I could ever offer you, which is why I encourage you to read the Bible so that you are open to His Spirit and the message it breathes.

Be the Rachel He Loves

In this chapter we're going to touch on four women in scripture. Let's start in Genesis chapter 29, where we're introduced to Rachel, daughter of Laban, and the desire of Isaac's heart. Jacob loved Rachel so much that he was willing to work for seven years in order to gain her hand in marriage.

That story got me thinking. *Am I that costly to my husband?* If given the choice today, would Michael work seven years to win my love? What about your husband? He may have been more than willing to do that on the day you said "I do," but are you still the radiant bride he adores?

I'm not talking about having a 23 inch waist, or the long flowing hair you once had—those things all pass away in time. I'm talking about the virtue you reflect, the qualities you own, and the value you hold in his sight. Are you worth seven years?

Reading a little further, we see that after Jacob put in seven years on the job, Rachel's father, Laban handed over her sister Leah to be his bride--not "Rachel" as promised in their original agreement. Reading through this story again I was reminded of my own marriage, and the woman that I've become.

Look at your relationship where it stands today and ask yourself, "Am I still the Rachel that captured his heart?" After two, three, seven or ten years, are you still the radiant bride that he vowed to honor and cherish that day? Or once the veil was lifted, were you somebody else?

This beautiful love story goes on to tell us how Jacob served yet another seven years for the woman he loved. I see that characteristic of Jacob in my husband, and I observe yet another love story. A man who has cherished me and worked for our family for twenty-three years, and a man who is willing to work 23 more. I'm humbled and grateful for a husband who accepts this work in progress and believes in our love enough to press on.

But what do *I* bring to the table? That's the question that rests on my heart. Am I being the help meet he deserves, and am I putting in the effort it takes to make a good marriage work?

Mature in Your Experience with Jesus

I hope to be the Rachel he loves, and I also hope to be a woman that offers my children the best that I have to give. By enhancing my inner beauty I can be.

It almost sounds odd to think that inner beauty takes work, but it does. It's more than just having a great personality. It's a process of building virtue upon virtue that requires patience and discipline on our part.

> *So don't lose a minute in building on what you've
> been given, complementing your basic faith with good
> character, spiritual understanding, alert discipline,
> passionate patience, reverent wonder, warm friendliness,
> and generous love, each dimension fitting into and
> developing the others.*

2 PETER 1:5-7, THE MESSAGE

Those are the characteristics that I want to see when I look
in the mirror, and I venture to guess that they are the same
characteristics my family desires to see in me.

In order to start enhancing inner beauty, let's turn our eyes
to the scriptures where Peter lays out seven virtues that shape
our character, while allowing God to work in our life.

But first of all, what are virtues, and how do they differ from
values? The basic difference is that values are the things that we
deem as important in life, while virtues are conformity of one's
life and conduct to moral and ethical principles (dictionary.
com). In other words, virtues directly affect the way we behave.

These seven virtues in 2 Peter, chapter 1 are:

- Good Character
- Spiritual Understanding
- Alert Discipline
- Passionate Patience
- Reverent Wonder
- Warm Friendliness
- Generous Love

By looking to a biblical example of Ruth we see one of the only
two women referred to as "virtuous" in scripture. The other is
found in Proverbs 31. Using their example, we can work toward
developing a wholesome character with a keen desire to grow.

Virtue teaches us that beauty isn't found on a cosmetic counter or a fashion runway, but rather in the strength of one's integrity and gracious character.

Let's take a closer look at each one:

Spiritual Understanding

The virtue of spiritual understanding must go hand in hand with acceptance of truth. It's found in those who love God, hear His word, and also live accordingly, whether it lines up with popular opinion or goes against the grain of society.

Alert Discipline

Reflecting on 1 Corinthians 15:58, we are called to a life of diligence and purpose. As Paul said, *"Therefore, my beloved brethren, be ye steadfast, unmoveable, always abounding in the work of the Lord, forasmuch as ye know that your labor is not in vain in the Lord."*

A life of contentment and peace is offered to us by the hand of His incomparable grace, but should we desire to be that willful servant, both conscious living and practice are required of us.

Passionate Patience

We all carry two bags—each and every one of us—one is packed with virtue, the other our faults. I'm talking marriage here, when I say that somewhere between courtship and the seventh year many women have shifted their focus from one of adoration to fault finder. We start to analyze, dissect, and over analyze the faults that we find, hoping to reshape our husbands according to our version of the perfect man. Living in harmony requires patience on both sides as we work to rebuild our view of one another.

Reverent Wonder

"According as his divine power hath given unto us all things that pertain unto life and godliness, through the knowledge of him that hath called us to glory and virtue."

2 PETER 1:3, KJV.

In this verse we see that we are not only equipped, but also called to glory AND virtue. Glory is living a reverent life that declares the glory of God in all that we do. When people look at our lives, they should have a positive view of the Lord. That's what *being* glory is, as it differs from *giving* glory to God. But then again being glory gives glory doesn't it?

Warm Friendliness

When approaching our husbands we can look to the biblical example of Esther, a woman who used wisdom and reference when she came to the king with her burden. In Esther chapter five we see that when she entered the king's court she didn't burden him with her petition. She showed kindness and respect without *expectation*, and in doing so received her husband's respect in return.

While some women look down on this philosophy and view it as archaic, the wise woman understands what true love entails. True love is giving without expecting return. It doesn't keep track of wrong doings. It doesn't expect perfection, and allows room for fault. It plants gardens where brick walls have once stood. True love is painful and pleasant, while perfect in every way. It's grace in action.

Generous Love

This virtue calls us to a life of sacrificial love. We teach our children to take the high road when the going gets tough, to walk away from a fight, and how it's more blessed to give than for one to receive. We enforce the golden rule of "love your neighbor as yourself." But we can't accept the reality that loving someone as much as we love ourselves means that we must be willing to sacrifice our own desires for their happiness.

May we strive to accept that truth and love the way that *God* intends us to love!

> *With these qualities active and growing in your lives, no grass will grow under your feet, no day will pass without its reward as you mature in your experience of our Master Jesus. Without these qualities you can't see what's right before you, oblivious that your old sinful life has been wiped off the books.*
>
> 2 Peter 1:8-9, The Message

CHAPTER FIFTEEN

R-E-S-P-E-C-T

WE'VE TALKED ABOUT WAYS TO LOVE AND honor our husbands, but since I've had several women specifically ask me for ways to show their husbands "respect," I'd like to get specific about it in this chapter.

In order to gain an understanding and move forward on the topic, let's take a look at the definition of respect. Dictionary.com writes *"Esteem for or a sense of the worth or excellence of a person, a personal quality or ability, or something considered as a manifestation of a personal quality or ability."* With that said, we see that one can respect a person without necessarily respecting *everything* about him. We can respect a person as a whole, or we can respect ideas and abilities that they have. In other words we can admire things about them, and we can acknowledge that they are worth something.

That's really what respect is all about--acknowledgement. People want to be acknowledged for who they are, their accomplishments, and the ideas they hold--men, even more-so than women.

Here's an interesting statistic: www.loveandrespect.com: *We asked 7,000 people this question: when you are in a conflict with your spouse or significant other, do you feel unloved or disrespected?*

83% of the men said "disrespected." 72% of the women said, "unloved."

That statistic is interesting, but not surprising; countless experts have been saying it for years. Even the media, feeds off these well-known desires, targeting their movies and advertisements accordingly. I love being loved, and although my husband doesn't say it, I can sense the appreciation he has when I show him respect.

So what are some ways that we can show them respect? Here are a few:

Let him take the lead.

Make your wishes known, but let him, as the head of your house make the final decisions. Joyfully accept the choices he makes. Grumbling, arguing, complaining or pouting are not becoming of a woman, and will turn your husband off.

> *Better to live on a corner of the roof than share a house with a quarrelsome wife.*
>
> PROVERBS 21:9, NIV

Have a good opinion of him.

Husbands have x-ray vision when it comes to our brains. They know when we truly value them, and when we're putting it on. If we're accustomed to judging every move they make, it's time to bridle our tongue, and grab hold of the reins on our thoughts. Focus on the good, let go of the petty judgment.

Notice him.

As women, there are times when we like to be noticed for the way that we look, while men usually prefer to be noticed for the things that they do. Start noting the things that he does, whether big or small, and let him know that you appreciate the effort he's made. For example, if you have a disagreement, and he apologizes to you, make sure that you mention his kindness later.

"Honey, I really appreciate your humble spirit. It meant a lot to me that you apologized," goes a lot farther than saying, "I'm sorry too." Kiss…kiss…kiss…

Don't get me wrong, the kissing part is great, but also take time to notice his effort!

Show consideration.

I've met a lot of mothers who show little consideration to their husbands when it comes to disciplining their children. Unfortunately, I've seen a lot of naughty children as a result. When Dad makes a rule like "No eating in the van," stick to that rule.

Your actions toward your husband are a living gauge to growing souls. They watch how we comply, and live accordingly. My husband has said things from time to time that I haven't completely agreed with when it came to raising our children. One instance in particular was when I arrived home from a writing conference to find out that: "Dad told us we don't have to do chores anymore!!" Apparently, he was having such a great time keeping house while I was gone that he decided to take over for the kids. Monday morning came, Dad was off to work, and the kids had stopped picking up after themselves.

Times like these call for a private meeting of the parents who work as a team. I make my request known to my husband, and together we weigh the pros and cons before going back to the kids with plan B.

Think highly of him.

It can be difficult at times to think highly of a man who's stretched out on the couch with a bowl of chips on his chest, a remote in hand and little to no contact with you--understood. We all have times when we're frustrated that our man isn't quite the prince charming we met years back when we were courting. I think that in many cases, we've both slipped--husband *and* wife. Dating had a way of bringing out the best in us. We dressed up for each other, we paid close attention to everything that was said, and we encouraged each other constantly with our words. It's important to realize that while we're getting comfortable we still need to make an effort to be the charming woman he met.

Flowers, dates, kissing in the back-seat of a car, and wearing designer jeans, does not a Prince Charming make. But being there through the birth of your child, working hard to take home a paycheck, bringing his family to church, and taking care of you when you're hurling over the throne, are noble features to be desired in a man. If he has done any or all of those things, he's worth a second thought. Start to view your husband with high regard, and you'll find much to be thankful for.

Reverence is Our Contribution

Now let's move on to "reverence," and see how it differs from that of respect.

I like to say that reverence is the granddaddy of respect. It's a deep level of esteem, coupled with the fullness of admiration. Without a word the heart whispers this message, 'I am solely devoted to you.' This is the attitude God commands us to have toward our husbands.

This is a great mystery: but I speak concerning Christ and the church. Nevertheless let every one of you in particular so love his wife even as himself; and the wife see that she reverence her husband.

EPHESIANS 5:32-33, KJV

While husbands are required to love their wives as their own selves, reverence is our contribution to laying the foundation of a Godly marriage.

When a man looks at his wife, he's looking for a reflection of himself in her eyes. A reflection that says, "I'm worth holding onto," and "I mean something to her in this world."

Does He Deserve Your Respect?

Showing reverence isn't always the easiest thing. We're talking about *human beings* here, who at times may disappoint and infuriate us. This is where we look past our duty toward man to see the perfection of Christ who gave up His life on the cross-- unfailing love abounding in grace.

I encourage wives to love and respect their husbands, because in doing so we become the radiant bride we were fashioned to be. I honor God when I honor my husband. I'm a crown of great worth when I'm intimately connected with him. And I radiate love when I live out my purpose, which is that of being his help meet.

But the question remains--and to many it's a valid question worth consideration--"Does your husband deserve your respect?"

The obvious answer is, not necessarily. He might be annoying, rude or obnoxious for all I know. But what I do know for sure is that God definitely deserves our respect and it's His will that we bless our husbands through the way that we live. God desires that we are a helpmeet, and with that desire, He has equipped each and every woman for the job.

When I wrote "Reshaping It All" with actress Candace Cameron Bure, I went into it with the initial expectation of being a co-author in every sense of the word. But when I deeply considered what was best for the book, I knew that it was necessary for me to step down and let her take the lead. It wasn't that she was more important than me, or that I was of less importance in the project, it simply meant that God designed each of us with different talents, and in order for our partnership to function at its best, I let Candace take the lead. By being second in command I've discovered a joy in working with her.

In the same way, I happily choose to be second in command when it comes to my marriage. I love that my husband is my provider, my protector, a godly example and wise leader.

If I asked you all to kneel down and wash your husband's feet when he got home from work, many women would be appalled that I am taking a step back from the progress that modern women have made over the past forty years. Even a photo of a woman kneeling before a man is unheard of, yet Jesus humbled himself to the level of a servant as he knelt to wash the disciples' feet. In John chapter 13, His act of humility teaches us to abandon our passion to lead in circumstances through which we are called to serve.

Foot washing is more than a beautiful ceremony, custom or rite; it's the life application of a soul completely surrendered to God.

> *In the same way, you who are younger, submit yourselves*
> *to your elders. All of you, clothe yourselves with humility*
> *toward one another, because, "God opposes the proud but*
> *shows favor to the humble." Humble yourselves, therefore,*
> *under God's mighty hand, that he may lift you up in*

due time. Cast all your anxiety on him because he cares for you.

1 PETER 5:5-6, NIV

Feeling respect for someone who's admirable can be a lot easier than showing respect to someone who's not. And let's face it, girls, there are times when we can all lose sight of the admirable characters our husbands once had.

CHAPTER SIXTEEN

LOVE AND LET GO

*Love him through those days when your
patience wears thin; search for his hand
through the sheets on a cold winter's night;
embrace him with arms that confirm your
passion runs wild; let go when you must
and allow him to fall.*

IN THIS CHAPTER I WANT TO address those women whose husbands are weak in the faith; whose husbands are unsaved; whose husbands aren't measuring up to their expected level of standard. And while I do, I'm also speaking to myself, as this is a lesson we can all glean wisdom from.

The Freedom to Choose

Freedom is something we all crave, because it's one of God's essential gifts to mankind. Adam was created in the image of God and that image came complete with the right to choose. Had there not been a tree of forbidden fruit in the garden, God would have eliminated the "choice" to *serve* or to *sin*. Adam chose *sin*. It's the same choice that we're given every day of our lives: sin or serve—which one will you choose?

But if serving the LORD seems undesirable to you, then choose for yourselves this day whom you will serve...

JOSHUA 24:15A, NIV

God knew that Adam would sin. He also knew the implications that this sin would have on the future of mankind and His Son, Jesus Christ, but rather than prevent Adam's choice He gave Adam freedom to choose, fail, and fall. Yes, freedom to sin.

If God grants us freedom to that extent, shouldn't we offer the same freedom to others? Choice is something we all get to make; whether it's the way one treats our bodies, what we use to feed our minds, the beliefs that fuel our faith, or the habits that mark our paths.

Pressuring your husband to lose weight, to go to church, turn off the TV, or to be a better father won't do an ounce of good in the long run. But choosing a healthy lifestyle, living out your own walk of faith, sacrificing your time for your children, and diligently praying for your family are all actions that *will*.

We all know how it goes--a little pouting can go a long way in getting what we want, and if that doesn't work then the nagging just might. Put your words aside for a season, live your life the way you want others to live, walk in paths of righteousness, and let your actions be his guide.

Have you ever met a friend who loved running, then suddenly found yourself on a treadmill? Have you ever had a friend whose weigh loss spurred you on to live well? Have you ever met an awesome homeschooling family that made you think, 'Maybe we should reconsider our method of education'...

Get the picture? These are just some examples that illustrate the influential power our actions possess.

Yes, we should all inspire our husbands to live better lives—and they us—but controlling behavior is the wrong way to do that. We were created to both think and act freely—to fall if we choose; denial of that right produces a hostile response.

I'm reminded of the day I took my father in for cataract surgery. Before the surgery the nurse put a little paper into each eye and warned, "Don't open your eyes for ten minutes, or it could fall out."

Of course for the next ten minutes all he could think of was that fact that he wanted to open his eyes. Closing one's eyes should be a relaxing experience, but peace wore thin when that choice was removed.

In the same way, you can allow your husband to choose his own actions and to be his own man, or you can burden him with the weight of your expectation. The choice is yours—push and shove, or love and let go?

> *A person may think their own ways are right, but the LORD weighs the heart. To do what is right and just is more acceptable to the LORD than sacrifice. Haughty eyes and a proud heart—the unplowed field of the wicked—produce sin.*
>
> PROVERBS 21:2-4, NIV

The Art of True Acceptance

What is acceptance exactly? Dictionary.com describes it this way: *To accommodate or reconcile oneself to.*

By accommodating we make room for his failures, and through reconciliation we reunite ourselves to him.

Changing ourselves is such a difficult task, changing another is an impossible one. We "accept" one as he is because self-improvement is his personal responsibility—not yours. By changing our focus we see where he excels and to put it bluntly—where we fail.

We all carry two bags—each and every one of us—one is packed with virtue, the other our faults. Somewhere between courtship and the seventh year of marriage many women have shifted their focus from adoration to fault finder. We start to analyze, dissect, and over analyze the faults that we find, hoping to reshape our husband according to our version of the perfect man.

Too many women bring HGTV into the marriage offering their husbands one extreme makeover: "He'd be the perfect man if…"

In order to change that way of thinking we need to practice true acceptance and keep applying it to our marriage. Here are three ways to do that:

- **Receive him with thanksgiving.** When we live in a state of gratefulness the faults seem less important while the good traits start to shine. I recently witnessed that in my parents when my dad was diagnosed with fifteen brain tumors. The reality that he was dying drastically changed their appreciation for one another. There was far more kissing, hand holding and hugging between them than there had been in over fifty years.

  Two days before he passed away two of my sisters and I stood in the doorway watching him embrace my mom and kiss her like she was the young bride he'd met over fifty years before. It was one of those top ten moments in my life.

- **Recognize his humanity.** The most common thread that I've seen in the failure of relationships has been the inability to recognize our human frailty in each other.

  Wives, our husbands are human beings not soap opera stars, rock stars, or runway models. They are pain and pressure, love and laughter, strength and weakness dwelling within three layers of skin.

- **Embrace his individuality.** If I had things my way, I'd probably have my husband walking around looking like a victim of "Queer Eye for the Straight Guy." I dare to wear fashion and I must admit I've suggested some radical outfits for him. But his taste in clothing is far different from mine. Our sense of fashion differs, as does our sense of humor and our sense of purpose.

  A husband may do things that don't measure up to your standard of appropriate behavior, like leave his dirty socks on the kitchen floor, bore your company with his drawn-out stories, watch too much sports, brag about his job, or exaggerate his stories so much that they're barely true.

  Does that embarrass or annoy you? It really shouldn't. Yes, many girlfriends would agree that you have a problem, if you should spill out the details of his baggage over coffee, but the problem won't go away until you realize it's not yours to solve. He is a separate individual who takes in the world according to each situation he's dealt, and processes it *his* way before letting it out. His quirks are *his*, and your quirks are *yours*.

With that said, let me also add that acceptance doesn't necessarily stand for approval. There may be things that he does which are against your moral or spiritual standards. It might even be an issue of not sharing your faith. There is nothing we can do in these situations other than realize that his actions belong to him. Live your life by example, and bring your prayers to the Lord. We can't change a person, but God definitely can!

> *Wives, in the same way submit yourselves to your own husbands so that, if any of them do not believe the word, they may be won over without words by the behavior of their wives.*
>
> 1 PETER 3:1, NIV

Submission Isn't Permission

Throughout the pages of this book, we've talked about accepting your husband for who he is, and submitting to him as the principal figure in your home. Before I close this book however I want to stress an important issue: submission isn't permission.

Let me explain. When I suggest that we accept him for who he is, I'm not talking about tolerating dangerous, abusive or illegal activity. What I'm referring to is the everyday annoyances that anyone deals with when they are living with another person and sharing their bathroom and bed.

I know that anytime we use the words "acceptance" "respect" or "submission" women who aren't willing to submit to the design of God's Word rush in to defend their feminism, and the accusations will fly. I say let it soar.

I was a victim of domestic abuse, and I know what it's like for a man to come home and brag to his wife about the people he has mugged on the streets. I've listened to stories of him, wearing a ski mask, chasing down a young couple with an axe held high in the air, assaulting one woman with a fist to the face, and one handicapped person with a blow to the head--secrets I kept safe for years. I've been held captive against my will; thrown on to the ground and spit on in public while people stood by and did nothing. I'm familiar with restraining orders, and all too familiar with pain.

So I will stand up to anyone who accuses me of supporting domestic abuse, but first and foremost I'll stand up for my faith, which states:

> *Wives, submit to your husbands as to the Lord. For the husband is the head of the wife as Christ is the head of the church, his body, of which he is the Savior. Now as the church submits to Christ, so also wives should submit to their husbands in everything.*
>
> EPHESIANS 5:22-24, NIV

Let's get past the mindset that submission equals permission and move toward a deeper understanding of God's plan for marriage. According to my understanding of scripture, the chain of command looks like this:

1. God
2. The Law
3. The Husband
4. The Wife
5. Their Children

Within that chain of command we are given a set of boundaries that must line up with scripture and the ultimate will of God. When we step out of that plan, we step out of the chain of command. Because I am in authority over my children, I do not have the right to abuse them or break the law. I am under submission to God, the law and to my husband, and therefore my sphere of authority is dictated by such.

My husband is under submission to God and the law.

> *Submit yourselves for the Lord's sake to every authority instituted among men: whether to the king, as the supreme authority, or to governors, who are sent by him to punish those who do wrong and to commend those who do right.*
>
> I PETER 2:13-14, NIV

Those rules dictate his boundaries. If he steps out of those boundaries, he steps out of my chain of command. **I must submit to God first, all else comes second.**

We see an example in Acts chapter five.

> *Having brought the apostles, they made them appear before the Sanhedrin to be questioned by the high priest. "We gave you strict orders not to teach in this name," he said. "Yet you have filled Jerusalem with your teaching and are determined to make us guilty of this man's blood."*
>
> *Peter and the other apostles replied: "We must obey God rather than men!"*
> Acts 5:27-79, NIV

So girls, just so we're clear from the dung throwing of the over-zealous feminists, let's be clear in saying that *submission* does not equal *permission*.

Illegal activity, including domestic abuse should be reported to authorities, and if you are in danger, you need to be removed from that situation and seek protection immediately.

There are places like Focus on the Family who have counsellors who are equipped to answer your questions and advise you on where you can go to get help. Call: 1-800-A-FAMILY

PART 2

PRACTICAL APPLICATION

SCHEDULE 1

Toss Out 25 Things

Before we get started on cleaning our home, I'd like to encourage you to begin with *less*, or for some of you—much less. There are things that we all have stuffed behind closed doors, hidden inside our drawers, laying under our beds, thrown onto our shelves, stacking up in our cupboards, crowding our counters, expiring in our freezers, hiding on top of our fridges, and squeezed into our jam-packed closets. In other words, we have an excess of junk.

Cleaning out my daughter's room, I was reminded of those times when I've seen doctors holding 20 pounds of body fat in their hands while the audience looks on in disgust. This is the equivalent to ugly fat, the only difference being that it's "lifestyle fat."

Our society gives so much attention to eating lean and shedding body fat, but little attention is made to living lean and climbing out of the pit of lifestyle obesity.

A few years back I went to Jamaica with my husband. The trip was a life-changing experience. I had never witnessed miles upon miles of poverty stricken homes before, but that week I did. My heart went out to those people when I saw that they were living in shacks no bigger, and less accommodating than my garage.

But during my stay there I witnessed something else. These people were dressed well. I didn't come across one person whose clothes weren't clean and well pressed, nor did I witness a beaten down culture. They were happy and content people who took much care with the little they had.

All I could think of on the way home was how much I wanted to purge my junk.

Shortly after that, I was inspired by a book called, "Throw out Fifty Things," by Gail Blanke. Gail encourages readers to go into every room of their house and get rid of things that have been hanging around for years. It might be an old tooth paste lid or the wrong shade of nail polish; it might be a jacket from 1997 or a pair of shoes from last summer. All of these unnecessary items are cluttering our closets, our drawers, and our life.

So I held an experiment of my own and asked my daughter to toss out 25 things. Within a few minutes my dining room table was full of stuffed animals, old shoes and a few broken toys. Less than fifteen minutes of work, and her bedroom already felt different.

I challenge you to try this today. Start with 25 things. It doesn't take long to toss out 25 things, but it does make a world of difference. And if you're anything like me you'll get back to work tossing out 25 more, again and again.

Here are 4 Guidelines

1. Hold onto things if you must for sentimental reasons, but if you're not using the item, either throw it away or give it away. A lighter load will bring a sense of peace to your home.

2. Keep things that you find pretty or useful. If it's not pretty enough to display and it has no use to you, why do you hold on to it?

3. If you have to think about it for a while, you probably don't need the item.

4. Don't feel guilty about getting rid of junk. Remember that there are plenty of charity organizations that can resell used items. Think of it as a donation.

Eliminating junk is one lesson I try to teach my children. We can clean the house daily so things appear tidy, but if we keep shoving more junk into our drawers and our closets, there has to come a time when we say "Enough—it's time to lessen the load!" Or better yet, "Stop buying so much."

Spend about fifteen minutes going through one room. That's it—one room/25 things. Now times that by the number of rooms you have and you'll see just how much of a difference tossing out 25 things can make to one family.

My kids definitely had a lot of garbage the first time we did this, but I noticed that they were more than ready to part with these items. One of our finds were two Build-A-Bears that we brought over to their little cousins, and they love them!

Once the kids started tossing out 25 things it turned into more like 50 for some, which was their choice, not mine. All I asked my family is simply this: "Toss out 25 things." That's good enough for now, we'll tackle the rest later!

SCHEDULE 2

ORGANIZING YOUR HOME

NOW THAT YOU'VE TOSSED OUT YOUR junk, let's start organizing your home. Regardless of how big or small your house is there is a place for everything if everything is in its place. That's what my dad used to say, and you know what? He was right!

I once had a galley kitchen no larger than 5 x 12, which meant that I either learned to be organized or I sacrificed standing room.

Our bedroom was large enough for a double bed and one dresser, with a closet too narrow for an average-sized hanger. The clothes hung at a bit of an angle, and since I didn't have all that much dresser space I hung up most of our things. There wasn't a single linen closet, pantry, or medicine cabinet in the house, but I knew I could make it work. Rolling up my sleeves, I got creative seeking ways to store toilet tissue, towels, and bed sheets.

I grew up in a household where everything had a particular place, and my sisters and I were taught to keep the established order. Mom and dad raised six girls in a small house that was always as neat as a pin, because my Grandma—mother of eighteen children—taught her daughters well.

An organized home eliminates stress and the need for unnecessary spending. We lost a pair of glasses once that cost us $150.00 to replace, when all the while they were in the bottom of the kids toy box. If we had less toys—and those toys were organized—we might have seen the forest for the trees. But then again, how can you expect a kid without glasses to see trees? *grin*

I've learned that the key to getting organized and keeping that state of order is to replace cluttered chaos with wise solutions. With that in mind, here are 25 organizing tips and creative ideas that I've gleaned from my family and friends. Maybe some of them can help ease your load:

1. Discard or give away unused items. You'll have less clutter in your storage spaces. If you haven't used an item in a year or two, you will likely not use it again unless it has sentimental value.

2. When it comes to kids—labels are a mom's best friend. I have labeled my children's dresser drawers so they know exactly where to put clean underwear, and where they can find it. Tops, t-shirts, pants, pajamas—they're all labeled.

3. Designate a "kid cupboard" for small children. We had a kid cupboard for five years in which we stored plastic bowls, cups, and dry cereal within their reach.

4. Use a sock basket. We have a sock basket in the house where all of the kids and mom's socks go. When we want a pair we go to the basket. It eliminates a lot of hassle on laundry days. And our basket is tucked into a linen closet in the hallway.

5. Put aside plastic CD cases and store your music in a CD wallet. Either discard the cases, or pack them in storage, or use them for kid crafts. They make great frames for kid's artwork!

6. Remove the handle from old rakes, clean them well (spray paint if you like) and use them to hang items on the back of a door: mittens and scarves in a mudroom, ties in a bedroom, large utensils in a kitchen, or tools in a garage.

7. Ask a local bakery if they have any large plastic pails. Many of them (especially those that are franchised) get them in with their cookie dough. I've had one for over 20 years, and I think it holds 33 pounds of flour. I don't worry about flour bugs, and I keep a scoop in the pail at all times.

8. When you buy furniture, look for items that hold storage. We picked up an antique hope chest several years ago, that we use as a coffee table. We keep all of our photo albums in there, and any important newspaper clippings, or interesting birthday cards are stored in there too. Last year my husband bought me a set of vintage suitcases that I stack together for an end table. I store my sentimental items in those.

9. If you find an old dresser, or you plan on discarding one, keep the shallow drawers. Small drawers like those from an old singer sewing machine not only look fantastic, but they go far in organizing items like recipe cards or sewing notions. Other shallow drawers can easily be slid under a bed. Remember the little galley kitchen I had? When we remodelled that kitchen I saved the original drawers and slid them under the bed.

10. Fill your garage walls with rows of hooks so you can hang anything and everything from bicycles to garden rakes.

11. Keep a small basket in the living room to store remote controls and electrical cables.

12. Place a wicker basket in your bathroom with rolled up bath towels. When towels are rolled they store better, and they give you more space.

13. Do you have items in your dresser drawers that you rarely use, but want to hang on to? Some items might include fancy lingerie, slips, pantyhose, camisoles or bathing suits. Store these items in a shoe box under the bed or up in the closet to free up space in your drawers.

14. Keep all computer disks in one CD wallet. Use mailing labels to attach important information such as passwords and user keys. (Do they even have user keys anymore?) Mine are all labeled with the original product keys and all programs are stored in one CD wallet.

15. DVDs take a ton of room on the book shelf. I know they're cute, but wouldn't it be easier to store them all in one wallet? Again use the casings for crafts.

16. Use baby-food jars to store:

- Pins
- Needles
- Buttons
- Paper clips
- Thumb tacks
- Nails
- Screws
- Rubber bands
- Beads
- Marbles
- Bobbins

Store these baby-food jars neatly by screwing each lid to the underside of a shelf. Remove the shelf from the wall, flip it upside down, lay the lids in two rows across and attach the lids to the shelf with small screws. Screw each baby jar in place and flip the shelf back over. There you have it—hanging baby jars, perfect for a craft room or work shop. I discovered this baby-food jar idea inside the shed of my last house. The older gentleman living there before us used them to store nuts and bolts. I think they're cute enough to use indoors!

17. If you have a mud room, get a large cork board to post appointments and other important reminders where the family can see them.

18. Take digital photos of your children's artwork, and print off small replicas to post on the fridge. Magnetic sheeting can be purchased to create the most adorable fridge magnets. Store the original artwork away for safe keeping.

19. Find small storage containers for use under the bathroom sink. Plastic pails may work well for your area as they are taller and narrow. Keep cleaning products in one, hair appliances in another, and toiletries in the third. It's helpful to have all cleaning products in one pail that you can pull out on bathroom day or easily carry to any room of the house.

20. Use bins to divide the floor space in your mud room or entrance closet. Mine is big enough that each kid has a bin for their own shoes, boots, hats, mittens and scarves. Mittens and scarves should be tucked into the sleeve of their coat, but when I'm in a rush, I throw it into their bin. On the top of my wish list is "lockers." I'm hoping to eventually get one for each member of our family but haven't afforded them yet.

21. If you don't have a mud room, store two bins inside

your closet. One for footwear and the other for miscellaneous items like hats, scarves, purses, and gloves. Clean this bin out whenever you get a chance, so mittens and scarves stay organized. It's a *temporary* solution to calm the chaos of overfilled closets.

22. If your house doesn't have a closet in the front entrance, hang hooks on the wall for the jackets and keep your eyes open for a small bench or trunk that has storage space.

23. Keep small wicker baskets in areas that act as junk magnets. Have the family drop their items into the basket so that when it's time to clean you can easily carry the basket and put items away.

24. Used coffee tins are great to store markers, Lego or crayons. Have kids decorate and label them for a sense of ownership.

25. If you and your husband are handy enough, consider building a drawer into the bottom of a staircase, or the bottom three steps. The space under the stairs is always too low for use anyway. It's a handy solution for hiding shoes if you have steps leading to a foyer.

SCHEDULE 3

HOUSEKEEPING SCHEDULE

*Note: This schedule can also be found
on my website: www.timewarpwife.com*

GOOD HOUSEKEEPING STARTS WITH A GOOD cleaning schedule. There's nothing like walking into a house that smells as good as it looks. When floors are washed, beds are made and dishes are put away, the family gains a sense of comfort in knowing that their surroundings are under control.

Being clean and organized saves you both time and money. When all things are put in proper order you don't have to spend minutes or hours looking for lost items. And when supplies are carefully organized, you can easily find them instead of replenishing stock. That's where a housekeeping schedule comes in handy. It keeps you on track and helps to ensure that all areas get your attention.

This schedule focuses on house cleaning. It does not cover meal planning, bill payment or personal hygiene. It is designed to get your house in tip-top shape each week and keep it looking that way.

Tackle one area of your house/day, and before you know it you'll have it sparkling clean from top to bottom!

If you're starting from scratch, then the first week or two will take up much of your time, because there may be areas that you haven't been cleaning on regular basis. But once you get a good deep cleaning done, up-keep will be a breeze!

Daily Upkeep

My sister Betty always says, when the dishes and laundry are done a woman is happy, but that happiness dissipates quickly if we don't make a daily effort to keep up those areas. Dishes and laundry are constantly in use, and therefore we must continually be on top of those jobs.

This "Daily Upkeep" section of the schedule covers the cleaning that you'll need to tend to each and every day.

Make the Beds

It only takes five minutes to make a bed. Five minutes goes a long way to making your family appreciate you and showing that you appreciate them. If your children are old enough, ensure that they make their own beds before school. Caring for the house is a great habit for all kids to get into.

Laundry

Depending on the size of your family, you may need to schedule anywhere from one to four loads of laundry/day. Start with two loads each day (Monday-Friday) and decide if you need to increase that number or not.

While the water is running in the machine, wet a light-coloured rag and wipe down the washer and dryer if necessary (keep a few on hand in that room). Throw the rag into the load. Set a timer so you don't forget to put the second load in. The timer is also necessary for clothes that are drying. Whether they are in an electric dryer or hanging on the line, we want to fold them as soon as possible to prevent wrinkles. And besides that—fresh laundry smells incredible!

Once they are folded, put everything away. Piles of laundry littering the couch will take away from the hard work you have done.

About line drying: I had a clothes line in my last house that ran from the back door to the back lane. I loved using it in the summer time. And each time I hung clothes, I felt like I stepped back into the '60s! Since moving to this house a few years back, we haven't put up a clothes line yet. However, I do try to dry sheets and towels and blankets on my deck railing when the weather is nice. It's not the best alternative, but it satisfies my craving for the outdoor smell.

Here are just a few reasons that line-drying is good:

We save money on electricity
The sun kills germs and therefore the clothes smell so much
  better
Dryers are more apt to shrink your clothing
The sun doesn't cause static cling
Hanging clothes is good old-fashioned exercise

While I was in Jamaica I noticed that nearly every house had a clothes line. So when I mentioned it to our tour guide, she told me that her doctor recommended line drying for good health. Makes sense since the sun offers vitamins and kills germs.

If you don't like the crunchy feeling that you get from hanging up towels and jeans, dry them 3/4 of the time on the line, and finish the load in the dryer.

Vinegar in the wash is also a great way to kill odors, even odors as foul as cigarette smoke. Don't worry about your clothes coming out smelling like pickles, the vinegar smell also washes away in the water and gives the clothes a good cleaning.

Wash Your Dishes

Empty your dishwasher every night, or put your hand-washed dishes away. This clears space up for the next day's activities. Keep on top of dishes that don't fit into the dishwasher and wash them as soon as each one is emptied. Pots, pans, plastic bowls and juice jugs can clutter a sink, and a cluttered sink takes the charm away from any dining experience.

Find a liquid soap with an aroma that's pleasing. It will make your dishwashing experience a more pleasurable one and your hands will smell great.

Every time you wash the dishes, also take a moment to sweep the kitchen floor.

10-Minute Tidy

In addition to your daily duties, which I will outline below, set your timer for ten minutes three times/day and tidy things up. You'll be surprised at how much you can achieve in only ten minutes time.

I like to do this after breakfast, lunch and supper.

This step is in addition to laundry, dishes, and shedding your junk, which we'll get to next.

Shed Your Junk

Again set your timer, but this time it's only for 10 minutes/day. Tackle any cluttered area that you desire and discard junk. Have one box for "giveaways," and another for "throwaways."(See "Toss Out 25 Things" for inspiration and guidelines.)

While you're purging, keep this rule in mind: if it isn't pretty, useful, or sentimental, get it out of the house. As for clothing, if you haven't worn it in the past year, you likely won't wear it again. If you're hanging on to clothing "just in case" you might decide to wear it, chances are you won't. The longer it sits in your closet the less likely you will ever put it on. Pack it up and give it to someone who will cherish it as much as you did the day you brought it home. Besides--how much clothing do we really need?

Lighten your load by giving away items that you don't necessarily need. Want—perhaps, but need—no. Having less stuff makes cleaning and organization easier and there's far less dusting to do!

Incorporate Routines to Your Schedule

Everyone's schedule is different and therefore one routine does *not* fit all. Choose daily routines that work for you and your family. It could be as simple as listing three cleaning chores for the morning and three more for days end. Don't overwhelm yourself with enthusiasm or you might tire out. Handle some tasks today, and others tomorrow--it will all get done in time.

Start a Journal

As I mentioned in chapter three under the section "planning ahead," it may be helpful to start a home maintenance journal where you can record your routine, keep track of this schedule, grocery lists, plan menus and keep track of important "to-dos."

A three ring binder works well since the pages are removable. Or you could go the route of a notebook. Target carries the cutest little notebooks, and of course I have a few on hand. You can't insert pages, but if you're creative you can always glue a little pocket onto the inside front cover to store coupons and grocery lists.

Brown kraft paper is the perfect weight for book pockets. Cut out a square, fold the edges under on three sides (about 1/3 inch), apply glue for the three edges and fasten to the inside cover.

Don't Get Sidetracked

One of the best things I ever purchased was a telephone headset. Mine broke about a year ago, but I received another one for a gift because my husband knows how I can't live without mine. Phone calls can be so disruptive when you have dishes to wash, and unless you're as talented as my friend Sandra, it's difficult to be juggling both. A hands-free headset is well worth the money if you find that telephone calls are tying you down. I roam the house with mine.

The computer is also a huge distraction for housewives today. It used to be that soap operas distracted women, but at least they were still able to turn up the volume and move freely through the house to get their cleaning done. Not so with computers. Facebook, Twitter, and Blogger are all things that draw my attention away from my home. I need to be cautious that I'm not too sidetracked when there is house work to be done. Sitting in front of a monitor will not result in a clean house, ladies!

Daily Schedule

Monday

Clean the bathroom/bathrooms. Wet a cloth and sprinkle soap onto the cloth, wipe down the bathtub, the sink and the counters. I use a hand scrubber to remove tough grime. Use one scrubber for the toilet, and a separate one for the sink, bathtub and floors.

While my sister was working for a professional cleaning company, she picked up an awesome cleaning tip from them. Instead of using a standard cleaning product, my sisters are now using powdered laundry detergent to clean their bathroom sinks and tubs. Keep a small box of it handy under the sink (but away from the reach of little children) and sprinkle a bit onto a damp cloth. It works great for removing bathtub scum. Since it's much cheaper than the standard chemicals I switched over too!

Paper towels are my best friend when it comes to the bathroom. After I wipe and scrub the areas with the hand brush, I dry them with paper towels that I can discard. I also like to hang on to worn out socks, or undershirts that I cut into pieces and use as disposable cloths. One pair of long underwear goes a long way!

Cleaning your bathtub weekly is important as a ring can build up, making it difficult to remove.

Give special attention to the floor. The area behind the toilet is a gathering place for filth, especially if you have little boys. Reach in with a moist hand brush, and wipe dry with paper towels.

Keep the soap and brush under the sink where you can easily touch up areas during the week.

Clean the mirrors with window cleaner* until you can hear them laugh—not hysterically, but they should give a chuckle.

Then use the moist paper towels to wipe down the door handle and light switch.

* See window cleaner recipe at the end of this schedule.

Look up. Is there a fan that needs to be cleaned? Check your shower liner. Is it time for a wash?

Don't forget to empty the garbage. Next time you're picking up cleaning supplies, find a box of great smelling fabric softener and throw a sheet into the bathroom garbage to freshen up the scent. It doesn't have to be a brand-name, it just has to smell good!

Remember, when guests are sitting on your throne, they have nothing better to do than observe what kind of a housekeeper you are.

Tuesday

Spend time in the bedrooms on Tuesdays.

Change bedding, and toss sheets in the wash. Note: if you purchase deep sheets, they won't pop off of the corners as often. If it's nice outside, try hanging your sheets and blankets outside.

Organize clothes, and dust off your dressers. Take a look in your closet to see what you can give away. If it doesn't fit, or you haven't worn it in over a year, there is no reason to keep it. Put as much junk away as possible so that all clutter is eliminated.

Keep DVDs, CDs, and jewellry off of the dressers. Keep one or two books on each bed stand and put the others away in a book shelf.

Clean the windows and mirrors, and occasionally wash your drapes. Wipe down window sills, and clean inside the tracking of sliding windows. They say not to clean your windows on a sunny day, and the reason is that they dry too quickly, leaving you with a streaky finish.

Empty space makes for a comfortable bedroom so do your best to shed items when it comes to the most restful place in your home.

Wednesday

Today is kitchen day. The kitchen is the hub of the family, so in addition to the daily maintenance you do, deep cleaning this room is necessary once a week.

Organize your pantry and discard old food. Repackage items that have torn or opened boxes, and consider storing them in sealed plastic containers to eliminate the threat of insects.

Empty and wipe out your refrigerator. Thursday is shopping day and you'll need all of the space you can get. If you leave this chore to doing once monthly, you'll find it's far more difficult to get done. Constant maintenance is the key to keeping a refrigerator clean and functional.

Fill a glass bowl full of water. Place the bowl in the microwave for about three minutes. This should be long enough to steam the inside of the microwave. Now wiping it down is a snap! (My sister says she skips the bowl and just puts a wet cloth in--even easier!)

Wash your counters and disinfect them. Note: vinegar is a great disinfectant, and since it's edible it's a friendly alternative to using chemicals on kitchen surfaces.

A little vanilla on vinyl flooring hides pet odors, but beware of possible stains. You might want to use vinegar on your floors too.

Have a coffee maker to rinse? Powdered automatic dish detergent is the best for removing coffee stains whether they are in the pot or on your counter. Just a little bit will do. It also works well to clean a stainless steel sink.

Wipe down your appliances and your cupboards.

Empty your garbage. And before you put the next bag in, throw about five bags into the bottom of the can. This makes changing the garbage every day an even easier task.

Organize one or two drawers. Here's the thing--did you realize that most women have the same odds and ends in their "junk" drawer? Yes, we do! Ask one of your friends, and you'll see. And if you took a minute to analyze the junk you'd also see that this junk can be organized into 5-6 categories. Grab a handful of large Ziploc bags group similar items in each. Do these items sound familiar?

Pens, pencils, erasers, markers, Scotch tapes, masking tape electrical tape, candles, birthday candles, matches, lighters, string, twine, shoelaces, keys, padlocks...

It's a lot easier to pull out a bag when you need masking tape then to sift through a drawer of junk looking for it.

It's also a good idea to designate a shoe box for warranties, instruction booklets, and important receipts. It only takes five minutes to find a shoe box today, but you'll save yourself all kinds of time and frustration in the future.

Once per month clean the inside of your stove.

Use the hose of the vacuum to suck up crumbs when you're cleaning the toaster, and also use the vacuum hose to clean crumbs from the cutlery drawer. (Yes--we all seem to get crumbs in there!)

Thursday

Thursday is grocery day. Plan your meals for a week and write down the supplies you will need. Check to ensure that you have an adequate stock of light bulbs, cleaning supplies, toiletries, and the like.

If you have collected any coupons during the week, put them in your purse.

Call your husband to see if there is anything that he needs from the store before heading out.

If you have errands to run, this is a good day to do them. Save time and gas money by grouping trips together, and try to schedule errands for this day as well.

Friday

Vacuum all carpeted areas and clean all other floors.* Pull the couches away from the walls and get behind them. Every second week, remove the cushions and vacuum the inside of the couch.

* Also see carpet cleaning recipe at the end of this schedule.

Grab a dusting rag or a bounce sheet and dust any surfaces that you haven't touched yet this week. Clean any windows and mirrors that haven't been cleaned yet this week. See any scuff marks on your walls? Try using toothpaste to remove them.

Several decades ago, my sister Betty decided to jump on her bed with a pencil in hand. When mom discovered the mess she had made, Betty was sent to her room with an old toothbrush and toothpaste. It all came off.

Saturday

Spend time with your family on Saturdays working outside. This is a great day to mow the lawn or shovel the walk, depending on the time of year. In summer, transfer your plants. In winter hang Christmas lights.

Check your front door. Does the welcome mat need cleaning? Does the wreath need replacing? Do your front steps need a shovel or sweeping? Consider what you want done, and use this day to do it.

Grab a garbage bag and clean out your car. Vacuuming and cleaning the interior should be done 2-3 times/year, but let's stick with home maintenance here.

Take one day/month to clean out the garage. You may ask your husband to help you if it's too large a job to take on yourself. If he agrees, spend the time cleaning with him.

Sunday
Take time to enjoy this day of rest with the family.

House Cleaning Recipes

Carpet Cleaner

- 1/2 cup ammonia

- 1/2 gallon of water

Clean your carpet with a rag or soft brush. Absorb moisture with a dry cloth. Also works on upholstery.

Note: Always test a small area first.

Window Cleaner

- 1/4 cup white vinegar

- 1/2 gallon warm water

- 1/2 teaspoon of liquid dish soap

Since newer glass is thinner, and therefore dries quicker, omit the soap and use vinegar and water.

SCHEDULE 4

DEEP CLEAN YOUR KITCHEN IN 5 DAYS

ANY NUMBER OF THE FOLLOWING STEPS can be done once/week on kitchen day, but if you are looking to get it all done at once and are willing to put in the extra hours, you can do them in five consecutive days for an overall deep clean.

Once the kitchen is deep cleaned use your judgment according to your lifestyle when deciding how often you'll repeat the steps.

Day One – The Cupboards

1. Empty out your cupboards (one section at a time if you're low on counter space) and put all items onto the counter top or kitchen table, just like you would on moving day.

2. Give each cupboard a good washing out with warm soapy water and a damp cloth. Wipe dry.

3. Get up on a step ladder--or onto the counter, if you're careful--and wash the top of the cupboards.

4. Take a look at your inventory and decide what items re-

ally need to be there, and which ones should go. There are only so many cups a family can use, but over the years dishes find a way of migrating into our space. Imagine that your kitchen is brand new and decide if these are the items that you want hanging around.

5. Take a look at your spices. Are they several years old? We all have a few spices that we've bought for that one-time recipe, but if they've been around over a year most of them won't do your food any good (with the exception of vanilla). I tend to hang on to mine longer than I should because I don't want to waste money. If you're not sure, smell it and see if the scent is weak. Let your judgment guide you.

6. Do you have old fondue pots, punch bowls, or crystal that's taking up space? If you rarely use them consider moving them into storage. If you have enough space, put these rarely used items up high.

7. It's wise to label the inside of cupboards or drawers if you have little helpers that put dishes and groceries away. Things as small as measuring spoons can easily be lost causing you undo frustration in the kitchen.

Day Two – The Drawers

1. Empty the drawers onto the counter.

2. Use the hose of a vacuum to clean dust and crumbs out of the drawers.

3. Wipe out each drawer with warm soapy water, and a damp cloth. Wipe dry.

4. Put items back in your drawers.

5. Consider items that should be organized elsewhere.

Can wooden spoons stand in a tall cup by the stove? Should scissors be moved to an office drawer? Would my cutlery fit better if I had a larger cutlery tray? Make notes on organizers you may need to purchase from the dollar store or Wal-Mart.

6. Use large Ziploc bags to organize your junk drawer and to divide items into separate categories

Day Three - Refrigerator and Pantry

The refrigerator and pantry really need to be kept up, as you don't want food getting moldy on you or spilt milk to remain unnoticed. An untidy pantry is a cause of frustration when putting groceries away.

So while you need to upkeep this area more often, you also need to do a more thorough clean when you can. Once every two weeks is a good rule of thumb, depending on the size of your family.

1. Fill an ice cream bucket with warm soapy water and take out a cloth.

2. Empty the refrigerator completely.

3. Wipe down shelves and remove any that you can for a good wash in the sink.

4. Once the interior is clean, you can start putting items back in.

5. Pull the garbage over and dispose of any expired food.

6. Use the warm water and cloth to wipe down condiment bottles, milk jugs, etc.

7. Once all of the items are returned to the fridge, fill the sink with warm soapy water, and a second sink for rinsing.

8. Wash all dishes that aren't being returned to the fridge.

9. Clear any clutter from on top of the fridge and give it a good wiping down.

10. Consider what types of storage containers you are lacking for proper storage and make a note to pick them up next time you are shopping.

11. Organize your pantry, keeping similar items together. Decide on a place for each and label the shelves if you must. Searching through the pantry for sugar, baking powder, or pasta only wastes time when a cook is busy. Labels don't need to be a permanent solution, but they are good for training the entire family on a system where everything has its place.

12. If your pantry is cupboard style with solid shelving, you'll want to remove the items and wipe down each shelf before putting them back in.

13. Discard any expired food.

14. Repackage any items that are making your pantry a mess like loose crackers or pasta.

15. If you keep things in the exact same place each time, you will be far more productive in the kitchen.

16. Plastic wraps, baggies, and foil may fit better inside a drawer than they do on a shelf, if you have room consider moving them.

17. Use small plastic tubs to store items that don't stack well on a shelf, like bags of pasta or cereal. Keeping several bags of pasta in one small sized bin on the shelf keeps things much tidier than loose bags.

18. Once the shelves are organized, sweep and mop the floor (if you have a walk in pantry).

19. Consider any storage containers that you should be using to keep bugs away from your food. Also consider any additional storage bins you can use. Don't skimp when it comes to storage bins, they are a blessing when it comes to keeping small items organized.

Day Four – Stove and small appliances

1. Make sure you're wearing old clothing, and have a pair of rubber cleaning gloves.

2. Double check to ensure that the oven is turned off and all elements are cool.

3. Remove any removable parts including the oven door. Removing the door makes reaching in so much easier.

4. Put knobs in the dishwasher or in a sink of warm soapy water.

5. Cover the area around the stove with old newspapers to protect your flooring.

6. To clean the stove top, boil a bit of water in a kettle and pour a shallow puddle onto the surface. Cover the hot water with a rag (in places that have tough stains) and let it soak in the heat for about five minutes. Wipe clean and rinse with a clean cloth.

7. Remove the stove-top wells. If they are too difficult to clean with water, put them inside the oven to be cleaned with oven spray.

8. Apply the oven spray according to the directions found on the can.

9. Once your time is up, wipe the oven clean. And rinse with a clean cloth. Put the wells in the sink and rinse with warm water.

10. Reassemble the stove.

11. Open the drawer under the stove. Remove all pots and pans.

12. Vacuum the interior of the stove drawer.

13. Wipe out the drawer with warm soapy water.

14. Replace pots and pans.

15. Wipe down the range fan.

16. Fill a glass bowl full of water and add about 1/4 cup of vinegar to it. Place the bowl in the microwave for about three minutes. This should be long enough to steam the inside of the microwave. Wipe the interior and exterior with a damp cloth.

17. Keep the vacuum hose handy when cleaning the toaster.

18. Empty the crumb drawer into the garbage, and then hold toaster upside down over the sink giving it a slight shake.

19. Vacuum loose crumbs from the counter top or floor.

20. Use a cloth with warm soapy water to wipe down any other small appliances, including a water cooler, can opener, blender or coffee maker.

Note: Some ovens get grease and grime between the glass panes that can't be wiped clean no matter how hard you try. Last year my husband and I took the oven door off and placed it on the island. Within about 60 seconds he removed a few screws, and I was able to easily reach inside to clean the glass. We had gone about four years with a dirty window until we realized that they are quite simple to open up. At least ours was!

Day Five – Floors, Counter Tops, Exterior Surfaces

1. Pull out the fridge and sweep behind it.

2. Mop the area with a warm bucket of water and a bit of cleanser (my favorite is PineSol for the smell!)

3. Repeat steps one and two for the stove.

4. Look at your counter tops and decide which items should be there, and which items are cluttering your space. Remove unnecessary items.

5. Consider any counter top organizers you may want and add them to your list.

6. Wash counter tops, using hot water and vinegar. Use a bit of powdered dishwashing soap on a damp cloth for tough stains. You might also consider wetting a cloth with very hot water and resting it on a stain until the cloth cools. This is one of my fastest and favorite ways of removing table top grime.

7. Most kitchen flooring should be washed with a simple solution of water and vinegar. If you are adding a product like a pine cleaner, go light on the solution to extend the life of your vinyl.

8. Use a damp cloth with warm soapy water to wipe down the exterior or your cupboards and door knobs.

9. Water and vinegar or Windex is great for cleaning the outside of a fridge. If you have stainless steel appliances, wipe them with long vertical strokes.

10. Wipe down the light switch with a damp cloth. Turn off the kitchen light, and you're done!

A Kitchen Prayer

Thank God for dirty dishes,

They have a tale to tell;

While others may go hungry

We're eating very well.

With home, health, and happiness,

I shouldn't want to fuss;

By the stack of evidence,

God's been very good to us!

~ Anonymous ~

SCHEDULE 5

DEEP CLEAN YOUR BEDROOM

The sleep of a labouring man is sweet.

ECCLESIASTES 5:12

BEDROOMS TEND TO ACCUMULATE STUFF, WHETHER it be clothing, jewelry, magazines, or leotards most of us have too much of it cluttering our drawers and our table tops. It shouldn't be this way. The bedroom should be the most relaxing room in the house—a place where you can retreat to when you want to stretch out, or snuggle with your husband on a cool winter's night. But there's nothing relaxing or romantic about a room that's cluttered and disorganized, is there?

I'm going to offer you 28 steps that will get your bedroom into the shape that it should be. Depending on the current state of your bedroom, this deep cleaning schedule could take you anywhere from one afternoon to a few, but in any case, the final result will be well worth your effort. I promise!

1. Start by taking the sheets, pillow cases and blankets off the bed and throwing them into the washing machine. Set the timer so that you won't forget they are there.

2. Take your curtains down and get them ready to go into the next load.

3. If you have blinds, wipe them down with a damp cloth.

4. Grab a flat sheet out of your linen closet and spread it out over the bed. This top sheet is going to protect the bed from dust and dirt, and prepare the bed to be used as a large working surface.

5. Bring a pail of warm soapy water and a rag into the bedroom. Also bring paper towels, window cleaner, and a vacuum.

6. Go around the room and take everything off of your dressers and end tables (entertainment unit too if you have one) and put all of the items on the bed.

7. Use a damp cloth to wash down all surfaces including the window sill, the bed frame, photo frames, lamps, clocks, door handles, light switches, and drawer fronts.

8. Decide which items will be returned to their places, which ones will be discarded and which items you should give away. Your table top surfaces should be pretty and functional—not cluttered.

9. File away paperwork that is lying around and discard or store magazines. Keep only a few books out and put the rest away in a book shelf.

10. Put CD's and DVD's away in CD wallets or storage units.

11. Dust remaining items with a damp cloth and return them to the table tops.

12. Has the timer buzzed yet? If so, transfer the bedding to the dryer and wash the curtains next. Better yet—hang the curtains outside to dry if possible. Be careful when

washing curtains that they are indeed machine washable. If not, air them outside for a while and consider having them dry cleaned from time to time.

13. If you have a ceiling fan, wipe it down now, before you vacuum or put the clean bedding back on.

14. Now that the bed is empty again, take the mattress off. If possible, turn the box spring on end and vacuum underneath it. This is a good time to rotate the mattress and get the floor beneath the bed cleaned at the same time. Doing this step twice a year is a good rule of thumb.

15. Put the bed and mattress back in place, and put the top sheet over the surface again.

16. Remove every small to medium item off of your floor and place them on the bed or in the garbage. What about the closet floor? Empty that too.

17. Take dirty laundry down to the laundry room.

18. Survey the items on the bed and decide which ones should be discarded, given away or put in storage.

19. Vacuum the floor.

20. Take a look at what is left on the bed and put the items away.

21. Empty all dresser drawers and end tables and put the items on the bed. This will include clothing and junk drawers.

22. Go through your clothing before returning items to the drawer. If you haven't worn a piece of clothing in the past 12 months, consider donating it to charity. Having less means less work in the future.

23. Take rarely used items of clothing such as slips, cami-

soles, and leotards and place them into a small box that
can be put up in a closet. This will free up drawer space
for necessary items. Or keep an eye out for a vintage
drawer at flea markets. These drawers can easily be slid
under the bed to store extra items.

24. If you are short on drawer space, store off-season items
in large rubber bins.

25. Wipe out the drawers before returning the items, and if
necessary vacuum them with the hose.

26. Once all of the items are put away, gather the four corners of the top sheet and bring it down to the laundry
room.

27. By now your sheets and blankets should be dry. Bring
them upstairs and make your bed.

28. Wash the windows, the mirrors, and any other glass surfaces with window cleaner and paper towels.

29. Finally hang your curtains up, put your laundry supplies away, and get ready to snuggle in the most comfy
room of your home!

SCHEDULE 6

DEEP CLEAN YOUR BATHROOM

WHEN I HEAD INTO THE BATHROOM to clean it, I'm usually expecting to have the job done within 10-15 minutes. And I do. After all, how long does it take to clean a room that's 8' x 12'? Not long if you've been keeping it up week after week.

But if your bathroom has been neglected for some time, you might want to consider going in for a deep-clean, and getting into those dirty little corners that you'd rather ignore.

I remember when I came home from the hospital with my youngest child. My sister Betty came over to do some house cleaning for me, while I recouped from a c-section. After spending about an hour in the bathroom, she emerged saying, "I haven't gotten to that wall vent yet--I'll do that tomorrow."

That's the day I realized that I had never come close to really cleaning my bathroom. There are so many areas that I tend to neglect on a daily basis, but having a deep-cleaning schedule that I can pull out every six months or so helps to ensure that those areas get the attention they need.

In the daily housekeeping schedule, I gave you some tips on cleaning the bathroom and keeping it up week after week, but in this schedule we're digging a little deeper. I'm going to empower you with 53 steps that will get your bathroom in tip-top shape!

Don't think there could possibly be 53 steps in so small a room? Well roll up your sleeves and you'll see:

1. The night or the morning before deep cleaning the bathroom consider whether you require a new shower liner, and if you can afford it, pick up new tooth brushes as well. If you can't afford to buy new, put your toothbrushes into the dishwasher where they will be well cleaned. For good oral hygiene it is recommended that we buy new ones at least every three months. Don't tell our dentist, but I tend to go longer.

2. When you are ready to get started, gather up any towels lying around and throw them in a laundry hamper or basket.

3. Pull up your bath mats and either put them in laundry, or shake them outside.

4. Remove the shower curtain and the lining, and bring all of the laundry to the washing machine. If you have window curtains in the bathroom, take them down too.

5. Today you are going to wash towels, the shower curtain, the liner, and the bath mats. Put a load in and set the timer so you won't forget it's there. If you are using a plastic liner that cannot be put into a washing machine, set it aside to be hand washed, or replace it with a new one.

6. Bring a laundry basket into the bathroom that can be

used to store shampoo bottles and toiletries while you work.

7. Remove all toiletries from the shower area, the window sill, and the vanity counter top, and place them in the laundry basket. Ensure that all surfaces are clear.

8. Place the laundry basket into the hallway while you work.

9. Spray bathroom cleaner on the walls of your shower, or apply cleaner to a damp cloth. (I'll refer to it in this article as a "vegetable brush"). Note: Powdered laundry soap works well as a cleaning agent in the bathroom, and it's less expensive than many bathroom cleaners.

10. Put on a pair of soft-soled shoes, and step into the tub.

11. Using a vegetable brush, scrub down the walls of the shower.

12. Using the same brush, scrub the shower head.

13. Use an old toothbrush to clean around the smaller areas that the brush can't reach, like around the tap handles and at the shower head joints.

14. If you have mold growing on your tiles, you can mix water with a bit of bleach (about a tablespoon) in a spray bottle. However—do not mix cleaning solutions EVER. I once used two different cleaning solutions on a bathtub, and it turned rust red. The entire bathtub looked like it was rusted out. I called the company and found a solution, but it was stressful and annoying to

fix. Avoid it.

15. Ensure that you clean all areas like built-in soap dishes or toiletry shelves.

16. Once the entire shower area has been scrubbed down, it's time to rinse. If your shower head is flexible, this will be easy, but if not, use a wet cloth to rinse all cleaning solution away.

17. Time to step out of the shower, and clean the tub itself. If you haven't already opened a window or turned on a fan, do so if possible. I don't want you passing out from the fumes.

18. Spray the tub itself with cleaning solution, or apply cleaning powder to a damp cloth. Use the vegetable brush to scrub away the bathtub ring and the standing surface. Even if you don't see the dirt, it's there, so clean this area well. Also give attention to the surface top of the tub, scrub away any rings that shampoo bottles have left behind.

19. Pull any hair that you see in the drain and dispose of it in a bathroom tissue.

20. Use the toothbrush to polish the drain area.

21. Rinse the bathtub well using a jug of warm water and a damp cloth.

22. Grab a few paper towels and polish the shiny surfaces.

23. Spray the cleaning solution into the toilet and around the interior of the bowl. Lift the seat and spray the un-

derside as well. Using a toilet brush, scrub all areas of the toilet including the interior, just under the inside rim, and the underside of the seat.

24. Flush the toilet and lower the seat. With a wet cloth or paper towels, wipe down the top of the seat and both sides of the lid. Lower the lid so you can also get behind there. Rinse your cloth out in the sink, and continue washing the toilet with a bit of cleaning solution (there may be enough on your cloth already). Wipe down the exterior of the toilet including the top of the tank and the base.

25. For hard to reach places such as the base of the toilet, use a long handled vegetable brush designated for bathroom cleaning. (I use these long handled brushes for cleaning everything!) Scrub the floor surrounding the toilet with a bit of cleaning solution, or if you are worried about your linoleum, use a vinegar and water solution. This is where paper towels are a must for me. After scrubbing that hard to reach base, I wipe the area with paper towels and discard them. If you can't afford paper towels, not a problem--hang on to odd socks that you can use as rags and discard when you need to!

26. Pull a chair into the room, and wipe down the light fixture and any wall vents with a damp cloth. While you're up there, wipe down the top of the vanity cabinet. That's an area that's usually forgotten.

27. Moving onto the sink. Spray the basin and the taps with a cleaning solution, or again use a damp cloth with powder.

28. Scrub the area with the same vegetable brush you used for the shower. Use the old toothbrush to get into the small areas around the taps. Use the vegetable brush to give the counter a quick scrub down. Note: Ensure that you label the toothbrush with masking tape for safety.

29. Rinse out the sink, and use a wet cloth to wipe down the counter and the taps.

30. Polish the taps with a paper towel. And if you really want to make them shine use a bit of window cleaner.

31. Speaking of windows, let's give the windows and mirrors a good cleaning, using the window solution and paper towels. I've loved hearing the windows laugh since I was about four-years-old.

32. If your load of laundry is ready, put the second load in.

33. Pull the laundry basket in from the hallway and decide which items will go back onto your surface areas. If you have empty shampoo bottles, this is the time to throw them out. Wipe dusty and sticky bottles down if necessary and put them back in their place.

34. Looking at the bathroom at this point, one might assume the jobs done, but it's not. The surface is clean, but we still have the medicine cabinets and under the sink to get to! Use the empty laundry basket to store items from your medicine cabinet. Put everything in there.

35. With a damp cloth, wipe down the interior shelves.

36. If you have old prescriptions that need to be discarded,

do not flush them down the toilet or throw them in the garbage. You can return them to a pharmacist for proper disposal. Some mommies put them into a dirty diaper and then into the trash can so that they won't be consumed by garbage pickers. Cat litter works too. I have to tell you something here, just so you'll see how truly human I am. About a year or so ago I ate something that expired in 1994. It was a bottle of antacid pills that I had hung onto for far too long (obviously!) Check expiry dates and discard items that need to go. You'll feel so much better with less "stuff."

37. Go through your make up at this time too and decide which cosmetics and which facial products you should keep. Mascara should be replaced after three months. It might be time to part with old lipstick, concealer, and eyeliner, but if you're not sure whether you've had it too long, Google the shelf life of cosmetics in your spare time.

38. Restock the vanity shelves with necessary items.

39. Consider using a cup on your vanity top to hold make-up brushes. I have a big red Starbucks mug that I'm using for makeup brushes, lip liners and eyeliners. It's like a pencil cup for my bathroom. Also consider picking up a toothbrush holder if you don't have one already. Anything you can display nicely on the counter gives you some extra vanity space. A soap dish is also handy to keep the bar of soap from sticking to the enamel, but I've been using soft soap at the sink for years now. I buy the refillable containers, and there have been times when I've diluted it with a bit of water because the kids

tend to take more than they need, and it saves us some money!

40. Once all of the items have been returned to the vanity or discarded, move to the cupboard under the sink. Pull all of the items out, and place them in the laundry basket.

41. Wipe down the inside of the cabinet well, and wipe it dry.

42. Decide which items you'll return to the cupboard, and which ones you'll discard.

43. As you're putting the items away, consider ways that you can organize this spot. This is a great place to use small baskets and plastic pails. Hair dryers and straightening irons can be placed in a small plastic pail for storage. Use a small basket to store hand lotion and body products, use a separate one to store cleaning solutions. Use another one to store your cosmetics. Use another for hair products. Having small baskets under the sink are like having a bank of drawers. Plastic organizers can be found at many dollar stores.

44. Once all of the items have been returned to the cupboard, wipe the laundry basket out with a damp cloth and head to the laundry room.

45. Fold the towels that you washed and keep your favorite one to hang up in the bathroom.

46. If you have a plastic shower liner to scrub down, you can place it in a sink of hot water with a little bleach

for about 20 minutes. If you're not one to use bleach, then use dish soap and vinegar. I've been buying a type of linen that almost feels like plastic. I throw it right into the washing machine when it's soiled. I find that buying a liner that costs a bit more saves me money and time in the long run.

47. Take the shower curtain and the window curtains into the bathroom and hang them up.

48. Using a damp cloth, wipe down the outside of the vanity cabinet, the towel rack and the toilet paper holder. Also wipe down the light switch, the door handle and the door frame.

49. Get a mop and a pail of hot water and wipe down the floor. If you want to use a pine cleaner for the smell, only use a bit to preserve the life of your vinyl.

50. Return to the kitchen sink and scrub that shower curtain. Rinse in a sink of warm water and squeeze out excess water.

51. Return to the bathroom with a clean towel and bath mats. Put them in place.

52. Hang up shower liner.

53. Turn out the lights, and you're done!

ABOUT THE AUTHOR

Darlene Schacht is an ordinary mom, living an extraordinary life, because of who she is through Jesus Christ. As help-meet to her husband Michael, she guides and nurtures their four children, leading them toward a deeper walk of faith.

Her work has been published in anthologies by Thomas Nelson, Tyndale Publishing and Adams Media. As well she has co-authored a book with actress Candace Cameron Bure, the award-winning and *New York Times* Best-Seller, *Reshaping it All: Motivation for Spiritual and Physical Fitness*. You can find Darlene at:

www.timewarpwife.com
www.facebook.com/timewarpwife
www.facebook.com/thegoodwifesguide

If you liked this book, please consider leaving a review at Amazon.

Printed in Great Britain
by Amazon

84874626R00098